Meaningfull
When Your Soul Meets the Ground

by Tiffany Kimbrough

paperback ISBN: 979-8-9858001-4-2

eBook ISBN: 979-8-9858001-5-9

Library of Congress Number: applied for

Winn Publications LLC, Texas

winnpublications.com

Meaningfull
When Your Soul Meets the Ground

by Tiffany Kimbrough

"Hold your breath, make a wish
count to three
come with me and you'll be in a world of pure imagination,
we'll begin with the spin
traveling in the world of my creation
what we'll see will defy explanation
if you want to view paradise, simply look around and
view it
anything you want to, do it.
Want to change the world? There's nothing to it
there is no life I know to compare with pure imagination.
Living there you'll be free if you truly wish to be
if you want to view paradise, simply look around and view
it
anything you want to, do it.
Want to change the world? There's nothing to it
there is no life I know
To compare with pure imagination
Living there you'll be free
If you truly wish to be"

Pure imagination, by Gene Wilder

How this book came to be:

It took me four years from the year of 2017 to 2021, to write this book. In the meantime, I was just filling pages upon pages of journals each year. Sometimes it would be three journals a year of notes, thoughts, prompts of how to know who I was, and where I was, and who I wanted to be. Sometimes it was just me rewriting what I've already learned...trying to clarify if I even absorbed what I studied. I think I was drawn to finally write this book because I wanted it to sit on my bookshelf before I died to be honest with you. But not only did I want that, I realized if there was one person out there who thought the way I did, then maybe this book will help him, her, or them. So here we are. This book is literally four years of notes and my thoughts. It's about ways to find yourself through tools, methods and practices that may help you throughout the entire journey of purpose/self-discovery or even just spark you to start. Whether you use the things mentioned throughout these chapters or not, this is a very suggestive book.

I personally started my journey of finding "Self", because I was just sick and tired of being sick, and tired of crying a lot. I was pregnant with my second child and living with my father for the first time in a while. I remember sitting there just tired of crying over everything and anything that made me uncomfortable. What I mean by "uncomfortable", is the fact that I just didn't have the answer to the ultimate question. Why in the **** am I here? Why did a Creator create me to just wallow and fail...sitting here not knowing why I even exist? What am I doing here? This feeling created anger towards everything I've learned growing up in the Church. So honestly, I ended up not wanting to have anything to do with a God who made me the way I was. Most of all, I was upset about the answers the Church gave me to confide in him when I felt at my lowest. It made no sense to not question further than what the Bible had answers to, but instead they would just say, "Have faith." Before I lose some of my readers, I want you to know I did not give up on God, what I did give up on was the process or the lack of processes in questioning God that the Christian religion has taught me. So, I began to search for a religion that allowed a lot more freedom and understanding. Long story short, I explored religions, practices, magic, science and anything that gave me more answers than what was already provided in my upbringing in the Church.

I tried everything and within all of it I began to see the puzzle pieces creating a bigger picture than I would have ever seen without this self-exploration. I am not saying that I found the answer to the biggest question on this planet, but what I am saying is that I found the greatest journey that a person can ever do for themselves. Now I'm not going to sit here and be like Christopher Columbus and say I discovered a whole new land when I didn't, there are countless books that say the same thing I say within these pages, but what is here is a person who is trying to encourage you to start. Start somewhere! Instead of just yelling this to a crowd of people every day, I have written upon these pages, trying to provide tools (whether these tools you already know or tools you never guessed would help you on your journey). Many of it is a bunch of hoopla, taboo, a little unorthodox and crazy. But we are all different, and so it's only right that we have so many tools to help us along a journey that is the most important journey on this planet which is finding ourselves. Finding our purposes. Finding our soul consciousness and allowing it to be a big part of us living life, if not our entire life. I am not the only one out there who has asked this question or questions.

The funny thing about this question about life is, we already have the answer and have run across it countless of times, but because of who we are as human beings, we like to complicate things. No matter how beautifully we were built we tend to make everything around us an entire blur of confusion and chaos. So, I will be meeting us where we are, by not changing years in an instance with a fix-it-all but by simply becoming a shoulder you can rest on for a moment as I talk your ear off about ways you can start your journey and exhale. Just imagine us sitting on a bench at the park indulging on ice-cream while we watch the day go by.

Let's talk about the Inhale of Soul consciousness.

Contents

Introduction

Dedicated to:

You. No matter how corny it
may sound, you matter and I'm
grateful you simply exist.

Introduction

We live in a world where the body and unconsciousness are the rulers of our everyday life. Then we ask questions like: Why am I here? What is my purpose? When we find some small sign of what it may be, we tend to put it in a box and label it, because that's what we're told to do. It may not be direct but trust me, everything is done for society so SOCIETY can make sure that they understand you, but unfortunately with that, you may not understand you. There is no possible way of putting a 3-dimensional being into a 2-dimensional description, but we sure do try our darndest. So when these questions arise, we really just run-in circles. We have run across the answers to many questions like these countless of times, and we tend to overcomplicate them. But the questions and the longing for the answers still remain! "Why am I here?! What is my purpose?!" In this we create a circle of life of confusion and restlessness. Leaving us grasping at straws to feel whole even if it is for a moment.

I am here to meet humanity where we're at, because god forbid we add more work to our lives. So, let's make the journey we are about to partake more adventurous, you can say.

Meaningfull is proposed to be a spark to what I hope to become an uncontrollable fire that burn down the reign of these "rulers" and put in its place, YOU.

Note from the Author

When referring to God, the pronouns that I choose are
of my own and nor is the name, or pronouns a limitation
to a certain belief system. I would also like to ensure that
when you are reading this book the usage of the word selections; purpose, soul, self-exploration, self-love, finding
one Self all equates to the overall journey that is being
illuminated here.

Meaningful
Definition: (adjective)

> 1. having a meaning or purpose
>
> 2. full of meaning

The one thing that will never leave humanity is our curiosity of finding who we are and our purpose on this planet. We constantly try to figure this out.

Let us sit on a bench together, exhaling from a long day and dig deeper. Maybe we will finally find the answers we long for. If not, at least unlock some doors. With every step, whether big or small, with every crawl, even if it only moves you a centimeter, you are getting somewhere. Somewhere worthwhile.

Self- exploration is what I believe to be the key of finding what you are supposed to do in this world, on this planet, in the physical realm, but I am not here to guide you to that purpose. Unfortunately, but also very much fortunate, you are to discover that on your own. Here I will say that your PURPOSE is being YOU. It sounds cliche and too simple, but it's true. Honestly, for some reason, we still struggle with the simplest of things...

"Saying something Cliché is basically something you already heard before but I'm going to say it again, it doesn't make what has been said any less than what it is." - Jay D Miller

I would like to WARN YOU that this book is similar to the harsh reality of what school really does for an individual.

I'm here to supply you with tools, but also like school, you don't have to use any of this in the future if it doesn't... in this case, resonate. For now, let's learn something new. Why not?

CHAPTER ONE

"All We need is love" **Love**

I started off with saying YOU (or you just by Being), is your purpose. Although simple, it is not enough for us, for some reason we need more! But that leads us here and we can start and end here, for Love is the answer.

There is a reason why human beings are favored with consciousness and more, when we were created. Maybe it is because we were made so intrinsically, with so much care and Divine love, that every part of our being wants to encounter every piece of this divine makeup. Now that's love, imagine creating something with so much care and time and then giving every piece of you, LITERALLY, just for your creation to be born, then for that same creation to discover every beautifully selected part of themselves. In return discovering you, and every bit of YOU within them. No matter your religion or beliefs, can we at least agree

YOU are existing; with a body, something called a soul, consciousness, earth beneath you and sky above? Can we agree that you matter enough to discover why you were put here?

"God is Love, Love is God"
Or
"Love is the Answer." Simple and straight.

We complicate what love is and what it looks like or should. I can say this, just like we are 3- dimensional, so is LOVE. Since we are Love, we must live it to understand it. But oh, how oh how do we try our hardest to define it. Let's see what we have...

What is Love?

According to Definitions from Oxford languages [just Google: love definition]

Love (n):

1. strong affection for another arising out of kinship or personal ties

2. affection based on admiration, benevolence, or common interests

(v):

1. to like or desire actively: take pleasure in

Let's look at some similar words:
be infatuated with, delighted, beloved, liking, weakness, partiality, bent, proclivity, inclination, keenness, penchant, fondness, dear, paramour, inamorata, inamoratos, querida, loved one, infatuation, intimacy, worship, adoration, passion, adulation, solicitude, kindness, fellow feeling, humanity, idolization, amour, intrigue, altruism.... just to pick a few out the group given to me.

Diggin deeper into "What Love is" ...lets compartmentalize it. How about the Four types of love.
- Eros: passionate love
- Philia: love of friends and equals
- Storge: love of parents for children
- Agape: love of mankind

Love has "languages" as well, The 5 love languages by Gary Chapman has brought people around the world to follow this way of thinking. You can either purchase a version of the book or take a test online by googling on the topic.

Here's a brief breakdown though...

1. Words of Affirmation-any spoken or written words that support, uplift in a positive manner.
2. Physical Touch-an act of touching someone (consensually) in a loving manner
3. Acts of service- doing for someone whether at random or when they ask, helping with chores or to-do list

4. Quality Time- being fully attentive in spending time with someone
5. Gifts- giving, whether making or purchasing something for/to someone

Let's not leave out the many suggestive memes! That we desperately lean on...

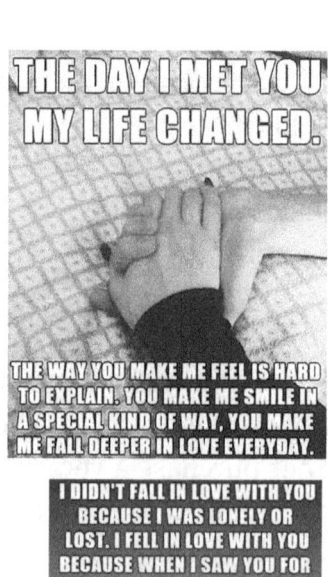

What does Love look like?

Okay, this is subjective, and we can agree on some things as a collective. I myself cannot sit here and transcribe a correct 3-dimensional definition on what love is and what it looks like. All I do know is that everything that has been said is true, but also when it stands alone from the other definitions it is "false". One definition standing alone is NOT the description of what Love is but maybe we can put a good amount of them together to get pretty damn close. What I do know is that self-love is important! So, start there.

Yes, it's true, you can't love anyone unless you love yourself first. Here is where and why love becomes so hard to describe, we haven't experienced self-love FIRST. No matter how evil started or starts in the world, we were made from love, so we are love! So stressing the matter of self-love makes sense, let's bring what we are made of to the surface.

I give you these answers that you probably already knew and if not, you could have Googled it. All and all we can say the definition is actually actively living your life and learning from it, that includes developing relationships with others. Yes, sorry but not sorry, relationships are the most beautiful teachers ever made. Always REMEMBER that your love for yourself is the ultimate key. I'm going to keep saying this until you understand it.

The Journey supplies

Self-love is a part of the journey and it will be constantly unlocked as you walk this journey to Self. Just like we are not able to learn what love is in one sitting, we cannot find all that is to self-love in just one part of the journey. As you begin and then later continue, you will find tools that'll work for you in discovering everything that is SELF...this journey is the intertwining of self-love, self-growth, purpose and just Being as a whole. It is interlocked, existing alone and in togetherness.

"Love only grows in love" by Osho Being in love (a great book to read.)

You are not going to just stumble onto Love and what it is. Even discovering how to go about self-love you would need to find tools or practices to help you on your way.

Here are some suggested tools and practices on discovering what Love may be; (with a tremendous focus on self-love firstly)

- Mirror work*
- Books/reading*
- Lectures on the topic
- Talking to the wise and older individuals*
- Picking up a spiritual practice(s)*
- Talking to yourself*
- Prayer
- Journaling

- Focused social media time
- Therapy
- Community groups
- Dating yourself*
- Dancing with someone or alone (alone is highly recommended)
- Active gratitude

Tools & Practices: Mirror Work*

Mirror work is a practice many therapists, counselors, psychiatrists, etc. suggest people do. Before we dive into what this practice is, mirrors can morph your look, so be careful and use different ones, if need be (If you have body dysmorphia, be gentle with yourself even more than already suggested) but make sure you designate at least one mirror to be your main.

Warning! You will get so accustomed to looking one way in your main mirror, that you need to be gentle with yourself when looking in other mirrors like at work or your mother's house. You may sigh a big "oof" or scream in shock like I did. Be kind to yourself, and make sure that the negative thoughts get pushed away as you are working through this exercise. For example, I chose to talk out loud whenever I felt inadequate in front of a different mirror by saying, "Today is not the day to address this," and I just kept on moving. In doing this, you won't end up destroying whatever work you already started through the exercise or be discouraged to start at all.

Mirror work is simply sitting in front of a mirror and

staring at yourself for a good amount of time. I would suggest 10 minutes at the very least each day, and if you get interrupted just go back or start over at a better time. I did my mirror work while breastfeeding my third child with two toddlers interrupting every three to five minutes. So, I get it. For the first several days just sit there, if your eyes wander, let them. You may come across negative thoughts like, "Yikes my eyes are asymmetrical, is that a double chin forming? Ugh the acne and the acne scars!" But don't let these thoughts distract you, go back to staring directly into your eyes and exhale. After the minutes in front of the mirror, make sure you journal your thoughts and feelings that you had during the exercise. List the things you disliked and ask yourself if anything can be done about it in the next several days, weeks, months, or years. Do not harp on the negative thoughts that occurred after doing all the work. If you find out that you can "fix" some things right away, go ahead. My overall suggestion is to be kind to yourself during the process.

One book that can help you with this journey, that I highly recommend, is Mirror work, 21 days to Heal Your Life by Louise Hay. This book will walk you through 21 days of mirror work if you need guidance, do what works for you. I am sure that there is something you can find over the Internet as well.

After the first week or several days, add focal points to your mirror work. Like, "I am only going to focus on the things I absolutely love about myself". Another day, add dancing in front of a mirror. Also, for a few days talk to your reflection as if you are on a date and then journal about it as if you were on an actual date. After a few "dates" write down what you wish you would have said or done on that date. Let's get a little bit crazier, next time pretend you got to the relationship stage with yourself, and start talking to yourself about your date and respond to it like you would want someone else to respond to it.

If you're sitting here reading this and saying this is too much to do, "This is crazy". OK, it's not for you. I mean you're missing out on the greatest few dates with a very special person, but that's your loss. Overall, this exercise will begin to help you acknowledge the inner voice and soul within, if not, it will get you ready for much crazier tools and practices that I recommend in this book.

Overall, there is so much to this practice. Make sure to look online for prompts or choose a book about this topic. Again, do what works for you.

Tools & Practices: Books & Talking to Yourself*

Books are an essential tool in self-discovery, self-love, and growth. I can recommend so many but here are a few:

- Meet Your Soul, A Powerful Guide to Connect with your Most Sacred Self by Elisa Romeo
- Emotional detox, Seven Steps to Release Toxicity and Energize Joy by SheriAnna Boyle MED, CAGS
- The Mastery of Self by Don Miguel Ruiz Jr
- The Mastery of Love by Don Miguel Ruiz
- Breaking the Habit of Being Yourself by Joe Dis-

penza
- The Warrior Heart Practice by Heather Ash Amara

Reading will promote the way you speak, will add to your vocabulary, and if you're anything like me, give you an unexpected pleasure that will feel like a full meal with dessert. But overall, it will get your wheels turning and your heart stirring.

On the topic of talking to yourself, whoever said it was an activity made only for the crazies, gave away all the fun for most of us, in exchange for us being "socially accepted". For some reason we fear to look crazy. In my experience, every wise person I know, talks to themselves. Having a conversation with yourself is only "crazy" when someone catches you, but I bet you that it feels good when no one else is around. It probably feels like your brain and heart gives out a big exhale every time. For those who don't feel comfortable, start using tools that allow you to feel like you're less crazy. You can use voice recording or even video on your phone. You can either walk around pretending you're calling someone, remember there are some rules to that: make sure your ringer is turned down low and no one can see your screen. But overall, no one will question you because nowadays we are doing everything on social media that requires some of these things. I mean, we already look crazy doing random TikTocs in public, so exercising self-love through this practice isn't much of a stretch and it's well worth it. Other things I suggest you can do, is journal and read it back to yourself.

When talking to yourself I believe your voice needs centering, and it's best to recenter against the walls of an empty quiet room where no other voices or vibrations can interfere. I can get into the throat Chakra and how this all works and heal your body in some ways, but let me just say it won't harm you if you wear blue or have a room decorated in blue where you can do the practice of talking to yourself. Or even eat some blueberries, or a blue Raspberry smoothie and when doing so, hum to yourself and listen. Disclaimer: If you are in LA or visiting be careful, please.

Tools & Practices: Actively Dating Yourself*

Well since I got you in the streets talking to yourselves, and if not, because you're avoiding that crazy hoopla so you won't add nine more cats to your home, let's talk about maybe taking yourself out on a date? Multiple ones and frequently.

First time in 31 years of my life I have heard it is embarrassing to go to the movies by yourself. Now look here, Sir or Ma'am, you are not going to sit here and tell me these lies. Even before having kids, I went to the movies by myself. Trust me, no one is looking at you and are laughing at the fact that you are by yourself. So stop looking back to see if anyone is looking at you, they are definitely not concentrating on you especially if they're sitting in the back, I'm just saying.

Now that I got that out of the way, we are here to talk about dating yourself. Go on an actual date by yourself. To the park, or to the bookstore, followed by lunch and a blue smoothie or green for the heart Chakra this time around, to the museum or wherever. Again, it would not hurt you. Maybe go to a crystal shop and look at these pretty rocks that may or may not contain energy although there's probably a scientific discovery that the Earth, including the rocks carry vibrations... I don't know, maybe a nice dinner or your favorite diner for a shake.

Warning! When alone, practice safety and awareness of your surroundings. Even text someone where you will be at if need be. Do not post your location when you are at that location, maybe wait till later. Do as I say, not as I do. The act of dating yourself will help you discover what love is, what it feels like, and will eventually overflow so much that you can't describe it, but you can give it. With this practice you are adding experience to your relationship with yourself and in combining the act of discovering yourself with actually doing things, it will create memories. Therefore, giving you something to reflect on every time you think of this journey. I can go into a deep discussion about how this works scientifically in the brain, but I will sum it up to this: it is said that creating experiences in a two-person relationship is crucial due to the fact that you will see the other person act in different scenarios; with different people, situations, and surroundings, and that's how you really get to know someone in full. So why not apply this to SELF?! Watching your actions and feeling whatever feelings you come across whilst doing this exercise will allow you to step out of the version of yourself that you see in your brain and actually see the version you project into the world. Whatever you dislike about what you are broadcasting into the world you can change, and align to what you want to express from within and bring it to the surface. This is important. Many of us are confused and feel highly misunderstood because we see ourselves one way and broadcast another version of ourselves to people around us. Aligning the 2 versions to your best version of self, is the only way to stop this unwanted self-trauma we unwarily create. So, grab some champagne or a beer and throw some petals down and begin.

Tools & Practices: Picking A Spiritual Practice*

Reading the Bible, actively attending Church and praying are great practices. My only suggestion to those who do this ALREADY is to stop for a week or a month. Unlearn how to pray and read, probably don't stop going to Church but instead, ease up on the attendance. Go every other week instead of week after week. While you have stopped, try a different method of praying and reading the Bible. For example, pray while standing, eyes wide open and pretend you are talking to God while you are cleaning your kitchen. When you read the Bible go to the back of the book and choose a word like, LOVE and read every suggested scripture on that, or randomly open to a scripture and read it. I'm suggesting this because, if you were born and raised in the Church like I have, a good percentage of your time is spent doing things out of habit. There is no harm in this practice. Taking time to shake off the old habits and finding your own way of worship and relationship with God is of the utmost importance here. Choosing a relationship in your own way of spiritual practice is another way of starting to find who you are and maybe your soul's purpose. This way of waking up your own version of practices is only a suggestion, and if you already do this, then great. Remember, it is OK if you end up still doing what you were taught, but now you're doing it because it resonates with you and not out of habit.

Now to the hoopla...

Other spiritual practices you can pick up are; Light language (also known as speaking in tongues), Tarot, meditation, mantras, moon rituals, focused manifestations (writing and then either burning it for fast manifestations or burying it for long lasting manifestations) or learning to read your Natal chart. Many of these practices have been adopted by other religions like Christianity already. I know you are side eyeing me and some of you are reading this in a crystal bath right now.

I have tried many spiritual tools and practices without self-judging myself and found what works for me and what didn't. Yes, I tried Tarot. It did not resonate for me although, I became an acquirer of different decks due to their beauty, and I may create my own deck with my art one day. I studied, learned, and practiced it for months, but it has yet to be a true calling to my path. Using different spiritual practices and tools with the focus on self-love and connecting to ourselves in general will awaken a soul consciousness by giving it a space to feel welcomed and acknowledged in ways that go way above our heads.

Let's dive deeper into the beautifully unstructured "crazy" of finding ourselves.

I have laid out practices that are a little bit more unorthodox to the human eye, but well worth it. Sometimes we have to step out of what we've been doing for a while and into something new to get to where we need to be. Actively and physically working on loving yourself is where you can find the definition of what love is. Remember, God made us out of love, the Divine wants us to discover what love is, and it's not that complicated although we make it. It's not that COMPLICATED because we are the answer. Self-love is the foundation of which this journey depends on, you cannot walk the path without it.

A nail is just a nail until a tool helps it serve its purpose. Find what works for you.

MEANINGFULL

CHAPTER TWO

Natal Charts,
the beginning of **the hoopla**

> What is Above is below
> But ultimately Within.
> We are all ONE.

Let's dive into what worked for me...

As you read, remember the topics that are being discussed are just suggestive tools. Like a hammer is just a tool, you can either use it to put the nail in the wall or find something else to do so.

Do you remember when you learned $2 + 2 = 4$, you weren't sure if it held any truth but nor did it harm you, and you accepted it. When you learn $1 + 1 + 1 + 1 = 4$ as well, you were probably an amazed 5-year-old who found that there was another way to find 4 and once more, you went with it. Then when you learned 9 - 5 = 4, you began to learn that there are many ways to get to the number 4, right? Well, there are many ways to get to know who you are. A math problem is just a bunch of numbers trying to get to a result, but you are more complex than that to rely on one answer or one way of discovering more about yourself, which is an extreme disservice that most of us tend to do. So, let's proceed with this "equation".

Natal Charts

Definition: noun,

According to the book, The Astrology dictionary cosmic knowledge from A-Z by Donna Woodwell, a Natal chart is an astrology chart that is a stylized map of the sky, predicting by position of the sun, moon, and planets as viewed from a particular time and placements on the earth. Or spiritual intentions of a given moment in time. The cosmic material in which an incarnated soul is clothed.

(Similar words: Birth charts)
"Wait, say that one more time I was walking my fish......."

The chart represents the Divine or Spiritual intentions of a given moment in time... it is the cosmic material in which an incarnating soul is clothed.

Don't leave, I promise simply reading this "Spiritual Hoopla" is not going to harm your beliefs. Come back, stick it out with me. We are just learning some tools that will either help you or just add to your understanding of you.
a Natal chart/ birth chart is:

- your birthdate
- the time you were born
- and the location of which you were born

Many people "don't believe" in zodiac signs. I say this lightly because once their birthday season come around or they see a post that favors their sign, it's always #Aries! #AriesGangGanG on social media. I also can see why their disbelief in it is very much valid due to the media and the publications of Horoscopes that generalize each sign without partaking in the fact that every individual whether they have the same sign or not, are different from one another. This disclaimer of how to receive the information is tragically not inputted, and when it is, we don't care to read that part. There are two other signs that accompany your sun sign. What I like to call this group is, your Trinity signs, also known as your Primal Triad.

The word "Trinity" may sound familiar; the father, the son, and the holy spirit. Let's all take this moment to realize, no matter the puzzle pieces they all make some connection to create a bigger PICTURE.

Look ma! God working his thing within me due to my foundational upbringing.

**"Give each child
a foundation with God
and you gave them the greatest gift."
In other words, once you see God
you can't Unsee or unhear him anywhere.**
Your Trinity signs consists of your sun sign, your moon sign, and your ascendant sign also known as your rising sign.

Definition:

Rising sign (also known as ascendant sign), noun

The Zodiac sign in which the ascendant of a chart is located, the rising sign indicates physical form, personal style and lifestyle.

Moon sign, noun

A Zodiac sign in which the moon is located within, your moon sign indicates how you feel safe   and comfortable, what your emotional outlook is, how you form habits and how the subconscious mind works.

For this definition there's a lot of focus on your emotions and feelings which leads me to summarize the moon sign to describe your overall temperament.

So, let's break this down using my favorite specimen, myself...

Now, if I only looked at my sun sign, Pisces, I would agree and disagree with some of the definitions and descriptions.

You're rolling your eyes now I can feel it.
You are probably saying, "Oh! She's a Pisces that
explains this book."

For example, I would say "Psshhh!I'm not a Pisces then. I don't think this stuff is right!" Now, now hold up, your sun sign (according to the website explore.mindbody.com) is your "identity", the expression of self. It is the essence that you shine out into the world. It represents the vital force that drives you to seek the highest expression of your true self. The sun sign is how you answer the question "I am" and how you experience life and express your individuality. In my own words, it is how you will take upon your purpose in the physical realm.

With adding my rising and moon sign I am creating a 3-dimensional form of my personality that I may not be completely aware of, but nonetheless it is written in the stars, and we have a tool in which to understand it.

To simplify the rising sign, let's say it's a "mask" people wear. It determines the way others see you and what you expect from the world around you. Usually like how one would see from meeting you for the first time. My rising is in Virgo, so you may meet me for the first time and say I'm a little bit OCD with my cleaning, very studious, independent, caring because I want to help you with your problems, and a bit critical. Oh yeah! Also, you may say, "She has a look to her that is clean and refreshing." Little that you would know, my Pisces sign is lingering in the background momentarily until the conversation continues or you meet me again. Where you later would see that I'm not clean all the time, my criticism is short and ends with a loving but contradicting statement, and I don't own an iron.

Now, the moon sign for the lack of better words, is your temperament. Your emotions and your feelings and how you respond to the world and the people in it. My moon sign is in Aries, keep in mind what I'm about to say doesn't apply to all Aries moon signs just like what I said about my rising doesn't apply to all Virgo risings. Shout out to Rih Rih, (Rihanna) my sun and moon sign twin. What an honor by the way, I'm just saying.

With my moon being in Aries, my temperament is quick to come and quicker to go but it is real, and it is my truth. So, it should be taken seriously. Please don't tell me how quickly I can stop crying after expressing myself. Those tears were real and that feeling I felt was even more real, the purest of my emotions.

"Fun fact" about Aries, since they are the first sign of the 12 Zodiac signs, they are the purest form of people. Like children who only can give out the purest form of themselves before being corrupted. Unfortunately, Aries people tend to fear this raw purity. As children, (actually, this pertains to all children of every sign) emotions are shaped to the comfort of how adults can receive it, and the purity of emotions are snuffed and stuffed down therefore affecting Aries more than less. Even if they are not aware of it.

Aries

"To you Aries I give the seed first so that you might have the honor of planting it. That for every seed you plant one million more will multiply in your hand. You will not have time to see the seed grow, for everything you plant creates more that must be planted. You will be the first to penetrate the soil of people's minds with My Idea. But it is not your job to nourish the Idea, nor to question it. Your life is action, and the only action I ascribe to you is to begin making men aware of My Creation. For your good work I give you the virtue of **Self-Esteem**"

"This is what God said to each of the Zodiac signs" by David Wolf

Although my statement about Aries children is not scientifically proven, this is one view of so many, the people of this sign are tough Nuggets for they are fire signs. I do remind you all, that they are deserving of a safe place to express themselves any way they want (in the confines of not harming anyone) with no judgment, and I promise you, you will feel the purity of joy.

All the Aries I know that helped me realize this:
- (My mom) Patricia Willis
- (My Dad) Wilton Kimbrough

- Damon Wilson
- Dizzy
- Adriane Powell

Looking back onto my moon sign, after you have met me and probably having a deeper conversation, by this time you have now experienced (hypothetically) that feisty, strong, and a little bit of the erratic responses I probably displayed in a moment of time. It probably scared you but also my rapid recovery and the finale that ended with a smile and a well suggested but firm "don't do that again." just made you oddly attracted to me or run for the hills. Either way I'll get over it quickly.

Let's pair all that with my Pisces sign which is creating my Trinity. Although I briefly described the sun sign, your sun sign will peek its head out in all encounters whether it's a first encounter, a deep conversation or at a glance. The sun sign would more than just peek its head out if it was put on a "stage" which also means, if it sits in a house. When diving deeper into understanding your natal chart this will make more sense.

"Imagine yourself as a musical in the theater, the House is a stage, the Planet is the character, the sign is the costume..." -Megan Powell

What my very much intelligent cousin means by this is, the House is one of the twelve mentioned below, the planet being; the sun, mercury, Venus, moon, etc. and the sign is the zodiac that sits within a planet.

"Example Chart: displaying here in this Natal chart; my Trinity, plan-

Your Natal Chart Report

Birth chart data for Tuesday, February 27, 1990 at
17:30 PM

Scroll down or click on a sign to learn more.

Name		Sign		House	Deg	Name	Sign		Deg
	Sun		Pisces	7	9.2°	Ascendant		Virgo	6.3°
	Moon		Aries	8	15.3°	House 2		Libra	1.7°
	Mercury		Aquarius	6	23.9°	House 3		Scorpio	1.2°
	Venus		Capricorn	5	27.6°	House 4		Sagittarius	3.8°
	Mars		Capricorn	5	21.4°	House 5		Capricorn	6.8°
	Jupiter		Cancer	10	0.8°	House 6		Aquarius	8°
	Saturn		Capricorn	5	22°	House 7		Pisces	6.3°
	Uranus		Capricorn	5	8.7°	House 8		Aries	1.7°
	Neptune		Capricorn	5	14°	House 9		Taurus	1.2°
	Pluto		Scorpio	3	17.8°	MC		Gemini	3.8°
☊	North Node		Aquarius	6	16.3°	House 11		Cancer	6.8°
⚸	Lilith		Scorpio	3	12.9°	House 12		Leo	8°

*The chart above uses the Placidus House System. To view placements in the
Equal House System, expand the chart wheel below.

ets, and Houses (first house being your Ascendent aka Rising sign)

What are Houses in a natal chart?

There are 12 Houses, and each house focuses on a different topic of life in each one. Within each House, it has a significant Zodiac that rules it. In your personal chart, it'll display the Zodiac sign that was apparent at the time and location on the day you were born. Stay with me, we are just staring at the number 2 in the math equation that will eventually get us to the number 4 if you decide to use this equation on your journey.

1st House

The first House is the House of self; self-awareness, the physical body, personality, appearance, personal views on life, self-identity, self-image, early environment, and beginnings.

Basically, how we initiate things and how we express our impulse. FYI, when we begin to talk about the other part of your chart, the planets, any planets in this House will influence your personality and how others may perceive you.

2nd House

This House refers to your own money and the material things you have, what you value, your hidden talents, sense of self-worth, self-esteem (sounds similar to the 1st house but it focuses more on how you value yourself, instead of describing your personality). The material things we are talking about here are everything except the house/home which is ruled by the 4th House. For example, cars, furniture, clothing, investments and securities, etc. The 2nd house focuses on how you increase and spend your own money (not other's money like in the 8th house), your attitude towards wealth and material possessions, and your potential for assembling it all.

3rd House

The third House focuses on communication. Also, siblings, neighbors, short journeys, and all forms of transportation. This House also includes the intellect, the lower mind (opposite to the higher mind focused on in 9th House) thinking patterns, and early education (before college). Communication includes messages, deliveries, the he said she said, phone calls, writing and reading.

4th House

The fourth House refers to the home, both the childhood home and the current home including; family, land, personal foundations, inner emotional security, your roots. (one's upbringing is associated with this House.)

"Hoopla" WARNING, for those who believe in reincarnation, the 4th House would show what karmic baggage you brought with you into this life. Even if you don't believe in reincarnation, you're likely to be surprised by what you find in this House. Here as well, whatever planets are in your 4th House affect your home life, your emotions, your subconscious, and more or less your relationship with your parents.

5th House

The fifth House focuses on children, the pursuit of pleasure and creativity. This includes personal interests, love affairs, sports, hobbies, risk-taking, teaching, creative self-expression, love given. This House is about you being yourself and loving it.

Romance, dating, love affairs, and sexual relationships are ruled by this 5th House, BUT marriage is assigned to the 7th.

6th House

This House refers to service, diet, health and physical sickness, physical ability to work, and employees. It includes volunteer labor, caretaking, and the mundane daily tasks. The 6th House really involves the quality of your work, the quality of the jobs you perform, not so much the actual career (career is in the 10th House). Examples of the daily mundane tasks include personal hygiene and our method of responding to everyday hiccups.

7th House

The seventh House is all about   one-to-one relationships: marriage, business partnerships, contracts, cooperative relationships, and also divorce, separation, quarrels, and open enemies.

The difference between the 5th House and this House is

that this House deals with the permanently binding relationships, whereas the 5th House refers to affairs that may be more temporary. Matters of the 5th House when starting to get more serious, we can then say that the relationship is moving into the seventh house. Try to remember 7th House relationships are about cooperation and sharing, and they generally serve some functional purpose in the larger social community like a marriage.

8th House

The 8th House rules what a relationship owns like joint finances and shared assets. (Remember the second House pertains to your personal finances). Also, this House governs death, taxes, inheritances, wills, legacies, sex (the actual act of sex), losses, personal sacrifices, etc. This House is about transformation and healing. The way to transformation and healing may require some type of loss or injury first. This House rules those processes and things by which we transform and become more powerful.

9th House

House number nine refers to philosophy, religion, learning, higher education, morals, journeys, travel, foreign countries and interests, spiritual urges, dreams, visions, higher mind, ideas, understanding and wisdom, books, publishing, ceremonies, and rituals. The 9th House is an area in which one will seek to discover the significance of larger fields of social existence through the mind by using analogy, generalization and abstract thinking.

10th House

The tenth House is the House of status, honor, reputation, and professional career. It's not about gaining "material stuff" like the second House. The 10th House wants success for the sake of honor and status.

This House includes authority figures, politicians. It also focuses on public areas of one's life, and the career that you grow into, as opposed to jobs that just get you by in life like what the sixth house rules over. Once again keep in mind, any planets in this house are very important.

11th House

The eleventh House is the House of community, friends or large groups. It refers to hopes, goals, ambitions, wishes, social groups, associations, humanitarian interests. It also refers to liberty, legislation and regulation.

12th House

The twelfth House refers to the subconscious. It illuminates the hidden self that exists within and apart from physical reality, the unconscious mind, subconscious memory, subconscious habit patterns from the past, mental illness, self-deception, escapism, spiritual realization, limitations, frustration, and down the line our self-undoing.

The Twelve Houses of Astrology
Aliza Kelly @alizakelly

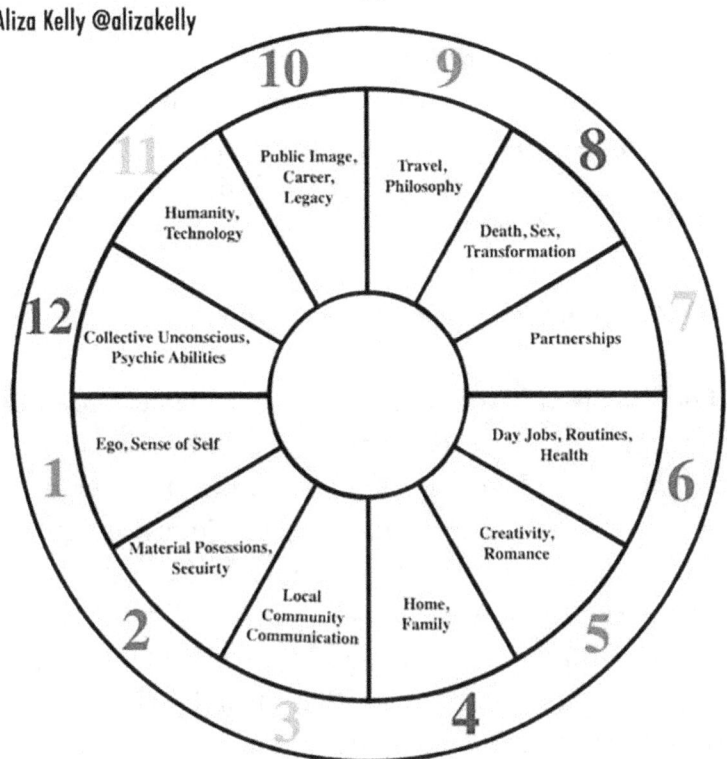

Physically this house includes things that take us away from daily life for example, institutions, secrets, and the lack of boundaries.

A brief description of what the planets focuses on;

- Mercury: logic, how you think and intellect
- Venus: romance, love, feminine energy, pleasure
- Mars: Aggression, sex drive, action and desire
- Jupiter: optimism and luck

51

- Saturn: boundaries, structure and responsibility (authority)
- Uranus: inspiration, individualism, rebellion
- Neptune: imagination, dreams, spirituality
- Pluto: transformation, death and rebirth
- Chiron: inner wounds of mind, body and soul
- Lilith: the shadow self
- North node: Direction of growth in life
- South node: Early Life, what you do instinctively

Looking at my own Natal chart, we can begin to understand what I'm about to say next. Within my chart you see different Zodiac signs in each house, now your chart can have the same sign in multiple houses. To further enlighten yourself on the topic, I highly recommend you research. How? The simplest way isn't always sitting and reading an entire book on the subject. In reality, I did but what helped the most was first finding out what my natal chart is by acknowledging that Google is your friend and the search bar is the key to your friend's home, use it. Once you find your natal chart, just take pieces and enter it into the search bar. Most websites you get your natal chart already have a description of it for you. But to take it in pieces is to simply enter in, "What does Leo in the south node mean?" into the search bar, or, "What does Mars in Aries mean?" You do not have to understand it in full in one day, in all honesty you will never understand it all in one day or even one year. I, myself, am still learning more and more every time I look at it.

Now look here, when we are looking at my chart, we are going with the fact that I got my information from one day asking my mother, "Hey mom what time was I born?", my actual asking was not because someone wanted to know if we were compatible or not, but instead for pure research that led to this book 4 years later. You, yourself can look up your time and location on your original birth certificate.

Anyone Remembers that one meme

**"My son texted me,
Son: Hey mom, what time was I born?
Me(mom): You stay away from that girl!"**

Now I learned about myself through this tool based on the memory of my mother and for 4years+ have been still learning myself with this info as my basis. Whether the time she gave me was slightly off or not, we can still use the chart. But I can say that I took my time and inserted different times from the time of 5 PM to 8:00 PM and discovered that no matter what time it was on that day (from 5pm-6:55pm) my Trinity signs, my planet signs and the houses 7 through12 never changed, apart from the time between 7:00 PM and 8:00 PM where the houses are shifted over which is a 2hr difference from when my mom confidently said I was born at 5:30pm. Basically, what I am trying to say here is that we're going to just roll with my mom's confidence in me being born at 5:30pm.

As you can see on my chart, there is the time and date

I was born. We're getting real intimate now. I'm going to show you something that helped me through my journey and self-acceptance by using this tool.

Now whether you notice or not, I will illuminate that my sun sign is in my 7th house.

If we were to apply the Zodiac being on a Stage aka House analogy, my seventh House (stage) in Pisces (costume) and it being my sun (planet) sign is something that I need to look at with the utmost importance. The 7th House with the sign, Pisces being what it is, together illuminates and focuses on relationships, mutuality, and sharing (shown in the chart above) which will promote and emphasize my character being a believer in true love and the one to save their partner (Pisces reference). This is only a snippet though. But through this placement I have learned so much in an area that had me confused! I began to realize why I date younger guys or did in the past due to the fact that they were in need in some areas of their life, that I probably already have gone through. Or there is some other reason why, but since this resonates with my truth, I will mark it as understood. Also, having this significant placement had me understand my desire for relationships, romantic relationships to be exact. This desire had a crippling effect on me that I saw throughout my life. Through understanding that the sun sign is more or less, of how your soul will project your purpose in the physical realm. My sign is sitting on a stage (House) of partnership, meaning my purpose has a lot to do with that. I have always felt the importance of romantic partnerships even when I was younger. Any other one-on-one relationships didn't hold a tremendous weight, but this may be different for you if you have the same sun sign in the 7th House like I do (although friendships belong more in another house as well). As I got older, I saw the speed up in my life when I was in a relationship. I was inspired to always move physically in my passions, or career when I was in a relationship, and it wasn't like my partner was pushing me in any direction. I just instantly felt inspired to do things physically that were on a path of connecting with whatever my soul wanted to broadcast to the world. Simply having someone there that I knew loved me, cared for me, someone I can talk to, to do things with when fun was needed and to share a life with, I began to just focus on other things that drove me to the direction of my purpose.

Overall, what my Natal chart said held some truth, on the stage of the 7th House my purpose was in action. My heart knew what my soul was trying to say in some way, "A serious partnership will help the purpose I am to do while on this planet," whether directly or indirect.

Now I said all this to say, one day I heard a woman speak on a podcast on the subject of natal charts. She simply said what I just said in fewer words. Basically, she communicated that once she found her wife, everything that she was and was going to be, began to propel her forward to the life that she was living at that time the podcast was airing. She is now an author, an activist for the LGBTQ+ community, and coincidentally she and her wife began to do a job together. She emphasized that her sun sign being in her 7th house was of importance. This may be nonsense to you but it extremely helped me with self-accepting my struggle on why every time I was single, I felt so stagnant in the world, as if the ground beneath me was pulled away and once again I was floating and dreaming of what's to come instead of actually doing stuff, like setting goals and accomplishing them. With that, I also felt the pressure of a society, which, at the time, was screaming that being an independent woman was important. "You don't need a man!" although very true, it wasn't a helpful rhetoric for my path and just caused an inner war of whys. After breaking this small but big cluster of confusion, I learned to exhale from a long feeling of suffocation and although I didn't like what I found out at first, the simple understanding gave me a gigantic step to wanting to discover more about myself. The simple act of understanding can move mountains or if not, give you the strength to climb it.

NORTH AND SOUTH NODES

Another thing I find amazing about this tool is that it has a section that will basically inform you about a small part of how your journey may look/feel. The North and South Node is what I can describe, as a "tell-all" of where you will dwell in from childhood and adolescents (South Node) and where you are going to "end-up" when you enter a point of maturity of adulthood and beyond (North Node). Using my chart as an example...

My South Node is in Leo energy and my North Node is in Aquarius. To find this out, you would look on your chart and find what your North Node is and then research your South Node by simply inputting your North Node (Google) and finding the opposing Zodiac Sign. Just search the South Node of [Zodiac Sign] North Node.

What my North and South Node mean for me is that, as a child and into adolescence I was very focused on ME; how I felt, how others made me feel, how I wanted to feel, and who was looking at me. My world was me oriented and I was always in shock when the people that were in my life didn't revolve around me. My purpose of life, I believed, was to be seen! I wanted to be an actress, but for some reason felt too extremely SEEN and would shy away...that is due to my Pisces sun, and no matter what the Node is trying to do, you may feel this conflict and confusion between what you want and what you need, as the two energies may push and pull against one another. Or in some cases, encourage one another. Now, I wasn't aware of this energy but as an adult looking back, oh yes, this was me. I would like to say that I am not describing Leos in their entirety nor am I describing everyone with a South Node in Leo either. I am describing small characteristics that I projected at that time that you would probably see in the description of the Zodiac Sign. The North Node which is usually activated at the age of 30 or when maturity hits at its peak, my North Node is in Aquarius. It being in that Zodiac means that I will have a sudden urge to want to do something for my community. Which is true, because at the age of 27 I began to feel this helplessness, I wanted to fix everything around me but didn't know how...and at that same time I was still stuck in my Leo energy, so with the combination I focused on what I could fix, which was me. As the years went on and as I went on with my journey of self, I grew more and more adamant about helping my community in some way...ANY WAY! By the age of 30 I had filled journals of everything I have learned to "fix" myself and now had thoughts of writing a book, starting a podcast, or SOMETHING! Here we are... in the actual mist of my North Node. Do you see...

I love this tool! Because of it, I sit with some knowledge and clarity on how my path may be, not only how it will put me into action of my purpose but also how to remain in purpose as I read more and more about an Aquarius North Node. Within this tool, the natal chart, I continue to discover more and more.

If this hoopla doesn't resonate with you, there are more tools that may, like the ones mentioned in the previous chapter, because relying just on a hammer to put a frame up perfectly onto a wall isn't enough.

A warning to all, be careful of what you come across, you may begin to open up old wounds and begin to shed light on some things that may make you feel uncomfortable. That's NORMAL. Keep pushing and be ready to understand the lows as you are trying to reach for the highs. Don't let the negative feelings stop you on this journey.

CHAPTER THREE

The Curse of Inadequacy is
the creation of confusion

Whether you truly believe it or not, you are special because you occupy a space on this planet for a reason, even if you don't know it yet. So, let's start with giving yourself little reasons to be alive.

I wish I would have known this way of thinking of giving yourself little reasons to be alive when I was younger or when I began to crave the knowledge of what my purpose was. Giving myself little reasons to occupy my time until I have reached clarity on what was to be done with my beautiful written DNA, would have saved me from so many tears, and so many failed attempts to meet my maker. Yes, I too struggled with depression. What matters now is that I am still here and reaching to stay within purpose?

"Little" Reasons

Little reasons can look like: being an above average student, being a parent, being the best employee, being a good boss, being a good friend, and so much more. Making those simple goals into a focus will probably consume some time until you reach clarity on a "higher" purpose or even find out that one of those "little" reasons is your purpose.

I realized my mother told me this in so many words and I just didn't understand it. Although she phrased it much differently, I now know the importance of these small focuses will help develop a beautiful journey in finding yourself, in finding what love is, and in my opinion, occupy a lot of time where depression allowed itself to be over the years.

Even if you haven't experienced depression, you probably experienced extreme lows sometime in your life. But now I ask you to ask yourself a question please, "Do I really want to stop living or do I just want to actually START living?" It took me three years after working on myself to ask myself this question. I realized my reasons for feeling like the soil of the earth will feel so damn good against my skin wasn't due to the years of feeling inadequate, but instead the lack of being in my purpose and in the life that I wanted. So, I sat and envisioned what would light me up with joy. Every time I have an extreme low, I would envision it again and again. With this practice, I realized I began to move into action. It still took me months but I can say within that same year, I saw my change from always feeling stagnant and inadequate to "OK, I'm talented," AND, "Maybe I'm just going to start writing and do some art". That's when the feeling began to expand into the people I actively chose to be in my life; what I was looking for on dating websites narrowed down, even within my family I decided how much energy I was going to put into different individuals. I also focused on the algorithm on my social media accounts by blocking some people and following certain pages that align to what I wanted to see in my life. Don't be afraid of any of this. It is challenging especially when choosing the frequency of communication you wish to have with different members of your family. Remember you can love people from a distance, even old friends.

(On the topic of how to consciously use social media, we will be elaborating on the topic at a later time in the book.)

StarGaze with me

The feeling of inadequacy is a curse in my opinion, no matter where it comes from whether it's programmed or written within our karmic journey. I believe it should not exist. As I stare at the stars written elaborately; named, described, put into elementals, planets, and focuses of habits I begin to see how maybe what we decided to put into the media about each Zodiac Sign has been slightly more toxic than we think. It doesn't discredit the tool at all but in using the tool I also felt the lows it can bring to a person. As you go on this journey of self using any tool, you will run across many tools that will show you the shadows of self, no matter what.

There is a great beauty in learning of one's shadow self, so that we eventually learn our bad habits and conquer them. What I have learned is that with the popularity of Zodiac signs entering people's beliefs, whether deeply or by passing, it tends to feed the masses a lot of the negative traits of each sign more than the good. Therefore I advise you to dig deeper and connect using the natal chart as a whole or bypass it all together.

What we have access to on the Internet about the Zodiac signs are not at their greatest when summarized. Unfortunately, we don't have thousands and millions of individuals who can understand or take the time to understand these signs. So, what is given is instantly taken as truth or completely written off, but if you choose to use this tool you may encounter lows due to its own faults and failures. When using this tool, I found out a lot about my sign, the Pisces, over the years I found that there are so many descriptions of Pisces that have been filled with negativity, in my opinion. Something that had me on the border of leaving this self-exploration and slightly wanting to give up on finding out my purpose. I ended up ignoring my sun sign completely at first and just continued learning by using other aspects of my natal chart for a while. Reading about a Pisces' natural ability to Daydream and escape, gave into a summation that added up as something tremendously bad. In doing this, it made me dislike who I was. To add upon that, when our deep emotions are belittled by being described as too dramatic and over the top, (which overall is a great quality due to it is just another way of saying Pisces are EXTREMELY empathetic) and our spiritual side is written off as mysterious/mystical and never to be further explained...continued this resentment I began to feel as I dug into "who I was as a Pisces". With those descriptions a passer byer would probably write us off, I WROTE MYSELF OFF! There are many signs that are described in a negative light more often than a positive one like; Geminis, Scorpios, Cancers, Taurus, but I can only speak for my sign and what I have discovered first. Surprisingly starting from 2021 I believe a lot of the "mystical" signs are being a little bit more understood and with that I see a gleam of hope.

The tools we choose on our journeys are not perfect and sometimes we can create room for bettering them as we learn more about ourselves.

Rewriting our "curses" into amazing qualities or simply taking our shadow selves and making it work within the light is something I'm glad to try to do here. It's hard to ignore after promoting my favorite tool in its own Chapter.

> *"Like a grand tree that can provide*
> *shade when the sun is up,*
> *our shadow self can too dwell*
> *in the light and know its place."*
> -tif *Down the Rabbit hole, we go* (coming soon)

To learn a little more on your end, the Zodiac signs have

an elemental group they each belong to, for example:
- Water: Scorpio, Pisces, Cancer
- Fire: Aries, Sagittarius, Leo
- Air: Gemini, Aquarius, Libra
- Earth: Taurus, Capricorn, Virgo

For example, Water signs are described as mysterious and very emotional whereas fire signs are sporadic and fast acting. The air signs, you would find them thinking of things that society may call taboo and find earth signs standing grounded on what already is and what is to come. They also have a modality to them....

Definition; noun
1. Modal quality.
2. A particular mode in which something exists or is experienced or expressed.

Cardinal:
  Capricorn (Earth)
  Cancer (Water)
  Aries (Fire)
  Libra (Air)

Mutable:
  Virgo (Earth)
  Pisces (Water)
  Sagittarius (Fire)
  Gemini (Air)

Fixed:
  Taurus (Earth)
  Scorpio (Water)
  Leo (Fire)
  Aquarius (Air)

A fixed sign will most likely be more stubborn about their beliefs and their way of going about their actions. Whereas the mutable signs are more flexible and open to views and beliefs all around them, sometimes they can fall into being wishy-washy. Lastly, cardinal signs are most likely to be people who enjoy being of service, but can come off controlling. It doesn't mean that you do not hold any of these other qualities if your sun sign resides in one of these groups, remember your natal chart as a whole will give you a full understanding of who you are and how you go about things. So, you may be a feisty (Fire) person who is extremely passionate about helping people off the streets (cardinal), a deep emotional (Water) person who helps people feel through an art piece on a topic you just learned about and expressed it well (mutable). Maybe a truth seeker (Air) who goes out to speak truths to those who may need to hear it regardless of the push back from the authorities (Fixed). Or simply, the understanding grandfather who ensures the safety of his family (Cardinal) and keeps the traditions alive (Earth)

Through 12 signs we have the deep divers, the beyond thinkers, the go getters and the well-grounded. All serving a purpose. One without the other, we will find this planet to be more chaotic than what we say it is now. No matter how dramatic, no matter how stubborn, no matter how far the thinking goes and no matter how quickly you make decisions... you are part of a system that keeps the love of humanity rising to the surface.

"REWRITING THE CURSES"

Let's start with David Wolfe's short writing, *This is What God Said to Each of the Zodiac Signs*

For Aries

I present the seed first to you so that you may plant it. For every seed you plant, it will multiply by one million. But you will not have time to watch the seed grow – everything you plant will produce seed that needs to be taken forth and planted again.

It is not your job to help each seed grow. What you must do is merely plant the ideas I present you in others' minds.

To help you accomplish this task, I give you the gift of self-esteem.

For Taurus

I instruct you, Taurus, to nurture each seed and nurse it into substance and health. This is a job that, no doubt, requires great patience, as you are required to finish that which has been started, lest the seeds be wasted.

To help you accomplish this task, I give you the gift of strength.

For Gemini

I grant you, Gemini, all the questions without answers. Your task is to pose these questions to the world so that they might ponder and gain a greater sense of under-

standing as a result.

To help you accomplish this task, I give you the gift of knowledge.

For Cancer

You have the task of teaching people to accept their emotions. Your life will be one dedicated to causing both laughter and tears in the lives of everyone you come across so that they might think and develop character. For this, I grant you the gift of family.

For Leo

Your job is to display My Creation to the world through your talents and abilities. You must be wary of pride and keep in mind that it is My Creation, not yours. If you forget this, people will laugh at you.

But if you do this well, I will grant you the gift of honor.

For Virgo

I ask that you examine all that mankind has done with My Creation. I grant you permission to scrutinize their ways and remind them when they falter.

To help you do this effectively, I grant you purity of thought.

For Libra

Your mission is service. Your actions will remind humans of their duty to others. This will help them learn cooperation and grant them the ability to reflect on the consequences of their actions.

To help you fulfill this task, I grant you the gift of love.

For Scorpio

Your task is very difficult. You have the ability to know what lies in the heart of others – but you do not have permission to speak about it.

There will be times when you are hurt by what you discover in others' minds and this may lead you to turn away from Me when you forget that it is not Me who is causing your pain but rather My task.

So why have I granted you this task if it is so difficult? Well, there is a plus side. You will discover your gift of purpose through this open-book look at humanity.

For Sagittarius

Sagittarius, I ask that you makc people laugh. Why? Because people tend to become bitter as they misunderstand Me and My ideas. But the laughter you provide them will turn their eyes back towards Me.

For this task, I grant you an infinite abundance of joy.

For Capricorn

I ask that you work hard so that others may see and be motivated to do the same. I grant you the gift of responsibility to help you with this undoubtedly grueling task.

For Aquarius

You are granted with the task of conceptualizing the future so that others may see and interpret it with as great a degree of skill as you.

To help you with this task, I grant you the gift of freedom.

For Pisces

Your task is the most difficult of all, for you must collect the world's sorrows and return them to Me. Your tears will be My tears and the sorrow you will absorb will often arise as a result of people's misunderstanding of My Plan.

But you will have the gift of understanding to pull you through this task.

All of you, my children, have tasks that I urge you to complete through your work and play, every single day.

David Wolfe wrote this beautifully in my opinion... and I would like to give a small message from me to those that I find to be the most misunderstood signs.

Airy Aquarius, although very misunderstood, I thank you for not caring to change yourself because you stand firm on unmarked, uncolonized land of Self. We as a whole will soon stand in understanding of the tiresome shift between these realms and upcoming realms that society is soon to reach in later years. We may not see them, but you do and we thank you in advance.

Dear Geminis, your interconnecting knowledge, the already known in the unknown merged into art forms has been proven to connect people to deeper selves. The uncomfortability you delivered this in, is beautiful because some of us choose to stay so comfortable that we never reach enlightenment.

My libra's, thank you for being the balance. The delay in your thinking or responses are of importance because whether we are aware or unaware, we depend on your judgment.

Fiery Aries & Leos you are "self-centered" in the best of ways. You give so much to others more than you see, so when you do finally take your energy to indulge in it yourself, it's only to replenish a soul that gives so much into the world that it doesn't notice. You spark joy no matter how it comes out. Whether it is a harsh reminder for others to be more optimistic, Aries...... or the simple way of living out your joy by just being, Leos.

Lastly my Scorpios, once on trusting soil of Self, the love and protection you give to what is around you, has a safe and guarded area to be free. Those who get the opportunity to be on that safe ground can reach opportunities that they may have never gotten without you.

Overall, no matter where any of these 12 signs sit on your natal chart, remember you are divinely purposed. The "dramatics" you read about is the ever feeling and ever flowing of emotions that allows you to connect to one another. That special ability, empathy, is important. That want of escapism is just manifestations that are not focused, so bring it to focus. That taboo thinking is only a threat to the narrow minded, you can see beyond the toxic program. That ever fleeting moment and once you adventure out is only an opportunity to connect and understand the world as a whole and return with riches of knowledge

WHEN YOUR SOUL MEETS THE GROUND

and experience. That "weird" way of expressing yourself is to show people, they too, have freedom to express themselves. That stubbornness is beautiful for it is the holder of tradition. The forever feeling of sadness is the grand key of transformation. Being hard to love is only a description from a person who was never meant to be your soul mate. Allow nothing to destroy you but allow everything to teach you. When reading these descriptions while on the journey of finding self, remember to always use it as a tool and not as the final truth.

You will have lows within this journey to Self, whether it is self-love, self-exploration, or finding one's soul's purpose. Whatever you want to call it, it is of importance to be kind with yourself. Curses can always be broken.

MEANINGFULL

CHAPTER FOUR

Beautiful PERSON-ality

We talked about the group of individuals who are our emotional artist who brings art to the world, the water signs. The go-getters who are the street lights to our dark nights, reminding us of joy isn't just beneath the sun, the fire signs. The reminders of our collective movement to the known unknown, the air signs. Lastly, our "did you knowers", the earth signs. Although I can do a whole book alone on Zodiac signs, let's jump into another tool.

Another healthy reminder is that, regardless of the Zodiac sign and their element or modality you fall into, you are a great make up of YOU, a personality to be reckoned with.

Your personality is a makeup of DNA and personal upbringings of your surroundings and the people in it, basically nature and nurture. Exploring your personality and how it fits into the world is one aspect of discovering self. Although putting oneself into a box can make you feel restricted in some ways, it can temporarily help you maneuver in this world with a little bit more understanding. I say temporarily not only because you don't belong in boxes but also because, as you grow older you evolve and change and with that, you would find different boxes that will describe you. Overall fitting into EVERY box but also in NONE at all! Like a plant that needs to be re-potted as it grows. This journey of Self is a continuous thing. The process will just get easier with time.

If the Hoopla doesn't fit your journey there are tools that carry more "facts" and studies that will help you discover more about you. Even if the hoopla is your thing, it doesn't hurt to see about these tools as well. One tool I enjoyed learning about is the Enneagram. This tool may appeal to more of the logical thinkers although it was derived from the teachings of the Bolivian psycho-spiritual teacher Oscar Ichazo. Which is a great reminder that the Spirit can speak to you in your way of thinking, there is no real separation from the soul and finding answers.

ENNEAGRAM

What is it?

The Enneagram is a basic personality test with nine different categories of personalities (numbered 1-9), each number representing a different personality type (no number is greater or lesser than the other). It shows the range of healthy to unhealthy behaviors that each personality type might demonstrate unconsciously.

The nine personality types described in the Enneagram are;
1. The Reformer
2. The Helper
3. The Achiever
4. The Individualist
5. The Investigator
6. The Loyalist
7. The Enthusiast
8. The Challenger
9. The Peacemaker

[Based on The Enneagram Institute]

- Type 1 THE REFORMER | The Rational, Idealistic , Principled, Purposeful, Self-Controlled, and Perfectionistic
- Type 2 THE HELPER | The Caring, Interpersonal, Demonstrative, Generous, People-Pleasing, and Possessive
- Type 3 THE ACHIEVER | The Success-Oriented, Pragmatic-Adaptive, Excelling, Driven, and Image-Conscious
- Type 4 THE INDIVIDUALIST | The Sensitive, Withdrawn, Expressive, Dramatic, Self-Absorbed, and

Temperamental
- Type 5 THE INVESTIGATOR | The Intense, Cerebral Perceptive, Innovative, Secretive, and Isolated
- Type 6 THE LOYALIST | The Committed, Security-Oriented, Engaging, Responsible, Anxious, and Suspicious
- Type 7 THE ENTHUSIAST | The Busy, Fun-Loving, Spontaneous, Versatile, Distractible, and Scattered
- Type 8 THE CHALLENGER | The Powerful, Dominating, Self-Confident, Decisive, Willful, and Confrontational
- Type 9 THE PEACEMAKER | The Easygoing, Self-Effacing, Receptive, Reassuring, Agreeable, and Complacent

The 9 personalities are typically shown on the outskirts of a circle and within the circle there are connective lines displaying "wings" of each designated "primary" number type personality. For example, my number is 7-The Enthusiast, so my connective numbers are 5-The Investigator and 1-The Reformer.

When taking the test, which you can find anywhere online, but the best test to take is the Riso-Hudson Enneagram type indicator (RHETI version 2.5), three number types will become your result. The first number is your primary personality type, this is believed to be your innate temperament. Although you are able to change and evolve over the years, this personality is to describe you at your most "primal" state. Along the sides of this type are two others that accompany it, and although sometimes contradicting, they complement and add important elements to your total personality (just like your sun sign, moon and ascendent sign in the natal charts). Overall, all the numbers are interconnected therefore we all possess a little of all nine personality types.

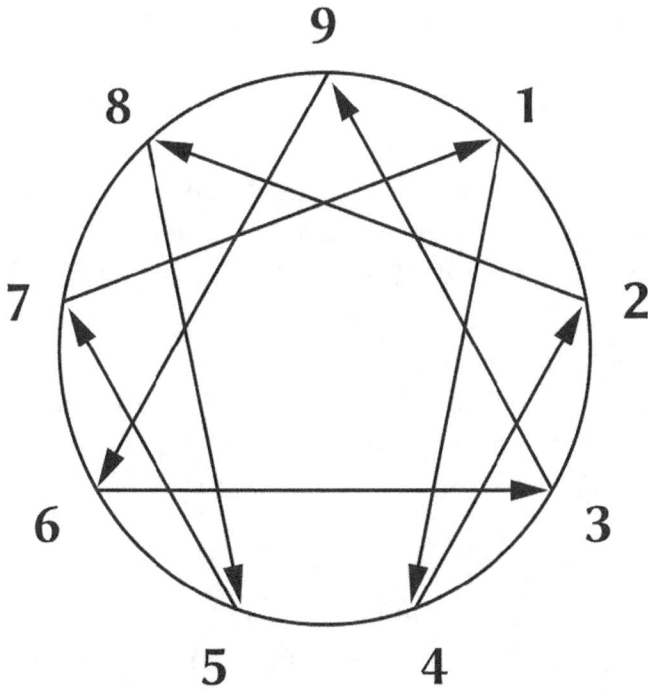

Within finding out your personality types, you will also find out where you base many of your unconscious reactions/responses on, whether it is Fear, Shame, or Anger/Rage. You also will find out some unique qualities or strengths in the way you express your actions; The thinking center, Instinctive Center or The Feeling center.

Instinctive Center/Anger/Rage: 8, 9,1 Type

The Feeling Center/Shame: 2,3,4 Type

Thinking Center/Fear: 5,6,7 Type

I am here to supply a new tool not completely to teach it, so if you are interested in this...please do some further research.

This tool was not made to box you in and be the final solution to what/who you are, but instead to shed some light on where you may dwell out of habit. Once exploring this tool many of the people who are a part of the Enneagram community like Russ Hudson, want each individual to take this information and discover ways to either strengthen or alter parts of their own lives. By no means are you supposed to adopt this tool as truth and bound yourself to it. I suggest this very same thing to all tools given to you in this book.

MYERS-BRIGGS

Another personality test, is the very popular Myers-Briggs test that is used by many companies around the world. According to the Myers- Briggs company's website, the Myers -Briggs test is a personality test that helps you identify your innate preference in four areas of personality.

1. How do you take information?
2. How do you direct and receive energy
3. How do you respond to the outside world?

4. How do you decide/come to conclusions?

Your results will be presented in the four Myers-Briggs preference:
- Extroversion/Introversion
- Sensing/Intuition
- Thinking/Feeling
- Judging/Perceiving

The personality type results may look like:

ISTJ	ISFJ	INFJ	INTJ
Introvert-Sensing-Thinking-Judging	Introvert-Sensing-Feeling-Judging	Introvert-Intuition-Feeling-Judging	Introvert-Intuition-Thinking-Judging
ISTP	ISFP	INFP	INTP
Introvert-Sensing-Thinking-Perception	Introvert-Sensing-Feeling-Perception	Introvert-Intuition-Feeling-Perception	Introvert-Intuition-Thinking-Perception
ESTP	ESFP	ENFP	ENTP
Extravert-Sensing-Thinking-Perception	Extravert-Sensing-Feeling-Perception	Extravert-Intuition-Feeling-Perception	Extravert-Intuition-Thinking-Perception
ESTJ	ESFJ	ENFJ	ENTJ
Extravert-Sensing-Thinking-Judging	Extravert-Sensing-Feeling-Judging	Extravert-Intuition-Feeling-Judging	Extravert-Intuition-Thinking-Judging

Each personality has its own description type. If this resonates with you or peaks your interest, I suggest you take this test and explore what you fall under. There are 16 types, we are not going to dive into every one of them, this book is a suggestive tool at its best.

Although this test is widely used for businesses and the dynamics in the workplace, many individuals use it themselves to dive deep into finding out who they are or to just understand themselves a bit more.

There are a lot more personality tests out there for those who are not with the Hoopla and have a more logical approach to things. Or if you want to combine them both you can. As long as you find something that works for you on your journey. If I haven't said this enough.

Some books I recommend on the topic are;
- *Personality Plus: How to Understand Others by Understanding Yourself* by, Florence Littauer
- *The Enneagram & You; Understand your Personality Type and How it can Transform your Relationships* by, Gina Gomez
- *Personality Type* by, Leonore Thomas

Whatever tools you decide to add to your tool box are your own and whether it helps you more or less than the others, at least it is getting you somewhere on this journey. The more you try, the more you will feel the ground beneath your feet.

CHAPTER FIVE

Foundated

Foundated- to be with a foundation. To be stable/ grounded within an area of life or most importantly within self.

By tif

I swore up and down that Foundated was a real word, or in the dictionary somewhere...but here we are....

At some part of our lives, we begin to crave stability or we finally realize once we become an adult, that stability is all up to us now. It is already enough that we must understand and try our damn hardest to create an environment that will shelter us, sustain us and keep us well-off... we do not need to be lost within ourselves. So, in starting this journey it will make you feel more "solid" little by little internally, that one day, not only will your body feel the ground beneath you but also everything within will wake up to this sensory pleasure. The journey within will begin to crave to find ways to continue itself externally.

As I mentioned in chapter one, I listed some practices and tools that may help on your journey. I want to elaborate on some more of those practices and tools and some others that haven't been mentioned yet. Putting more dirt beneath our toes as we no longer look down at our feet while we walk this path. Now that we know there's a ground that has been there this entire time. Time to look up and move forward, one foot in front of the other. Time to interact as we continue to feel our soul in every crevice of our being.

To add to the above book list (in chapter one) I also suggest the book called, *The Laws of Spirit, a Tale of Transformation, Powerful Tools For Making Life Work* by Dan Millman

This is actually the book that started my journey on finding who I was and why I was here on this earth. This is what led me to many other tools and ways I found out who I was. It brought me to the union of my soul and how it should live with me in this realm, we call life. If reading or audiobooks are not your thing let me suggest once again a few other things that might work for you, being:

> Sit with the elders- take out time at a family dinner or party to talk to grandparents, great aunts or even your parents to ask some questions about them, like what they wish they knew earlier in life, ask them about their hobbies, careers, jobs, etc. In ask-

ing questions, you can watch a played-out life of a human being (like a movie), succeeding and failing but overall living regardless of the circumstances. You can extend these talks to any person who has lived so many years on this planet, that includes; teachers, pastors, counselors, older coworkers, and even at a retirement home while volunteering.

You'll be amazed at how much information and insight and inspiration you will feel after talking to them.

Where you came from, your DNA- look up your culture, ethnicity or even your family origins. With this you can look into something that leads up to your very existence whether its DNA or history. Knowing one's heritage, bloodline and or even, the origin story of where you live may spark some insight on who you are and why you are here. There are methods on getting information about your family origins nowadays. There are advertised ways of getting this information through DNA testing and also you can use photos and any heirlooms passed down from generation to generation that holds a story and make sure you use tools that will gather more information. The internet, libraries, museums...

Alters- the more spiritual way of going about this is, you can also build an altar whether it's for your ancestors or for seasonal reasons and even for moon phases that occur weekly/ monthly. This will allow you to have a physical interaction with a realm you don't always see. Inviting this type of method into your life will invite things of the unknown so be very careful and do enough research.

I myself have a small altar after the passing of my grandparents to keep me in remembrance of where I came from. In some way, I keep them even near me within my home. It doesn't have to be something big at all, my alter contains a small miniature fountain that no longer works, with pebbles inside, a gold hippopotamus, a nerd Hello Kitty pin to remind me that I can always be myself, coins, and a ring passed down to me from my mother given to her from my grandfather, and on occasions, freshly picked dandelions. Which carries great significance that reminds me of my grandfather. I did this unexpectedly and realized what I was making once it was done. By no means did I know what I was doing when I started, to be drawn to things and begin to create this altar was very much unconscious, but once I did, I felt a great connection to Self through it. Soul guidance can be crazy but beautiful.

I also do random seasonal altars that I am drawn to. My way of coming across this tool wasn't that I researched it first, but instead was drawn to creating centerpieces that had tremendous focus and energy as I was creating them. So, you can say my soul needed to do it without even my mind understanding it. Once again, it was not until later that I understood what I was doing and then furthered my research that allowed me to understand it a little bit more than just doing it. When it came to the moon phases, I decided to continue building alters but I did   research before creating these specific ones.

> For moon phases and seasonal altars, I suggest you do your research and move within your own spirit to see which one works for you. There is no real wrong way or right way of creating these things. In my opinion, if your focus and meaning of doing it is done in light it'll create light energy but once again be wary of how you go about doing these altars, I still suggest research. By no means am I doing these things out of worship of anything but instead these altars that I am suggesting are to allow you to connect through action with your spirit and physical realm. Just like Church being something of the physical realm putting spirit and soul into a focused place, this is just another way of giving soul a place to dwell in the physical realm more.

In all actuality all these tools are to help surface souls more often than not, so that it may activate its purpose in the physical realm. Don't worry though, sometimes your soul will begin to naturally overflow into the external realm on this journey and there's really no stopping it. It may not be in this way of doing this but maybe another...

> **Numbers**-Diving into the spiritual realm of things a bit more, you can begin paying attention to numbers that keep recurring in your life. I say this be-

cause of my own journey and many others' who had the same occurrences. We all know about 1111 and making a wish every time we see it. But I realized after a while I began to see other recurring numbers like 444 and 808. My curiosity led me down another rabbit hole and every time I saw these numbers, I would immediately look them up just by Googling them. With the habit of seeing the number and looking it up I began to see other numbers and looking them up as well. Whether you believe in what the numbers represent or not, the messages speak loud and clear to the soul. Trust me, to this day I find it crazy but something within me is reading the messages loud and clear. Sometimes you have to feed the soul even if the body and mind does not understand it. Also, it doesn't harm you to always hear messages like, "We are near and helping you through your path, you keep going, you are on the right path," or "What you are thinking now is important focus on what your thought process is and be careful and always be positive," even 666 means something different than what we are taught in the Church. But I won't get into that.

Gardening/Adopt A plant- during 2019 through 2021 and probably beyond, a lot of us adopted plants and gardening as a hobby to get us by the first outbreak of COVID-19. Although I started it before this outbreak, I found having plants or a garden is an awesome method of getting to know oneself. Just like becoming a parent of an actual human being that you learn to be a better person, a plant in some ways, can do the same. To nurture a plant, it may get a little bit tiresome and feel like failure, but getting back up again and trying again will teach you so much. Plants teach you that you can be resilient, that you need as much nurture and kindness as anything else in this world, it will also show you if you are patient or not, and if not any of that, simply watching it grow for the time that it has been in your care will make you feel quite good. Something great was said by the man who created Black Men with Gardens on Instagram in 2020 (but I didn't discover until 2021), that a plant is your growing partner. This was beautifully said by Nelson ZePequeno. As you are growing, it will grow with you, although on individual "paths", you may find that connection beautiful and inspiring to keep moving forward.

Sometimes this journey will feel lonely, so imagine something is sitting in your corner, gently whispering, "Me too," or "You can do it, look at me...we're doing it." A plant can be that something. Being a plant parent can be very rewarding during the Journey. Do your research, start off small and with easier plants. One activity you can do is name a plant after yourself, and as you water it and tend to it...you are subconsciously taking care of yourself. Especially when or if you adopt the practice of talking to your plants. As you speak to them, those words will travel to you when you call it by your name.

> **Using social media**- using the platforms that we used to socialize on a daily basis, and even watch more than we watch our TV is a beautiful method to use as a tool of self-exploration. Looking up You-Tube videos on the topic of soul, purpose, self-love, self-growth, and whatever is needed to understand yourself is a beautiful way if done properly. And when I say properly, I mean not settling on the videos that you're looking up as your truth. Please take what resonates, and always do your own research. Also using social media platforms like Instagram, Twitter, Facebook and others through their provided tools on each individual platform can be another way of using it for exploring self. I will elaborate more on how I use and suggest other people to try out on using social media platforms like Instagram in the next upcoming chapter.

I can go on and on about which tools and practices you can start or continue on your journey with, but for now, I hope that I gave you enough. Hopefully now the ground beneath you feels a little bit sturdier or if you're like me, you actually feel it. This is where we're at, this is where we need to be to begin the next journey of living with soul abundantly on the surface of our life. We go day by day just living and for some of us, just to survive. But when we allow the soul to be so present in our daily life, literally, that is when we begin to know purpose and live it out in this world, in this lifetime. Putting our imprint not just on the surface of the earth but seeded into the soil also, to never be removed, forever reminding us that soul is a big part of LIFE. And with that, maybe we can call that our legacy.

SOUL SURFACING
ABOVE THE SKIN

In these next couple chapters I will be trying my best to show the importance of allowing your soul to take part in your daily life, and in your daily LIVING. Not only should we give it a place to dwell in, like Church, but most importantly allowing it to be the biggest part of your life by just BEING. Unfortunately, we allow our mind to control our daily lives. Sometimes we allow society and the government to tell us how to live our life purposefully. Going to work, going to school and being a great student, getting into college, being a part of sports, having a social life, buying a car, trying your best to find a career, raising your children, being a parent, getting married, dating, working out, buying nice clothes, buying great shoes, making your home the most beautiful, buying a house, paying your bills, eating, and once in a while enjoy life through a hobby or an event. This is all great in some ways, but it consumes every moment of our lives. Our minds have nothing to say about this because our minds live in habit. It has no function of individuality unless it learns it. The soul is the provider of such a thing. Your DNA and your environment may create an individual unlike another but it no longer lives as if it is separate from another human being.

I enjoy the forever journey of finding one's Self (self-exploration, self-growth, self-love, discovering one's soul and Purpose). It should be a highly suggested "hobby" everyone continuously dab into, more often than not. Many of us would say things on the lines of "I just can't find the time" or "I feel lazy when I do things other than what needs to be done" and some would find this too self-centered. Well, I want to help you find ways to include this very important journey into every moment of your life, it'll never really need time taken out of whatever you do on the daily because it will be embedded into time itself.

I do want you to know that taking time out to meditate, read a book, learn something new or do any of the suggested tools and practices in chapter one are IMPORTANT, not only for your journey but even for your well-being.

MEANINGFULL

CHAPTER SIX

Taken'd Time

Although the mentioned practices and tools in part one of the book do not take much time out of your life...they do take time. Here I would like to really focus on things that REALLY will not take any seconds or minutes out of what you are already doing on a daily basis anyways. The intertwining of soul and body on the daily will remind us we are a soul with a body experience and not the other way around...

Talking to yourself

We have mentioned this before in this book, but I would like to elaborate on how this is something that isn't as crazy as you may perceive it and how effortlessly it can be intertwined into your daily life.

Many of us have or had grandmothers who sang in the

kitchen and even at times talked out loud, conversing with someone whether it was Jesus or themselves. Even with seeing it, we still know and call our elders wise regardless of the continuous random conversations they have with the "air".

We ourselves are kind of guilty of this habit. Some of us probably find ourselves talking to the radio, songs, our plants, pets and even to movies. We talk out loud to something more often than not. And if this isn't you, I highly suggest you start.

The benefits of talking to one's self other than the fact that it can easily fit on your commute to work or school is that, you have the freedom to talk about anything freely without any outside judgment. That freedom will allow the purest of self to roam outwardly with no reservations. The first time doing it, you may restrict yourself but then you may release every cuss word and mean thought you have about anything and everything that you see around you. Just allow yourself to see where your thoughts would go and hear what you have to say with any emotion you chose to display. Of course, down the line, you may begin to not enjoy such heavy negative vibrations some cuss words hold and no longer feel like anger is the emotion you want to see yourself in anymore, but those days of PURE freedom you gave to yourself allowed you to free some pent-up energy and acknowledge that you don't want to be "the angry person". It's a funny thing that Freedom can help you discover about yourself.

After a while you may dab into all emotions and all

thoughts and eventually find out, not only your voice, literally because you may not like that your voice is too high or too low and you may realize you're speaking through your nose and your throat instead of your gut...but the version of you that never had the opportunity to surface in full. This may happen simply because you talked out loud and in doing that, you brought conversation to a place where you have full freedom. All these small discoveries will begin to form a "new person" and this "work" was done without taking out time from your daily task.

Listening

Listening is a key that will unlock many things within this journey. Actively listening is actually the most important thing you can do for others and for yourself. I challenge you to sit down with someone and simply listen without any response. If you're anything like me, this is the hardest thing to do. If you ever get the feeling like you are restraining yourself to speak or to respond to things and in doing so, you feel tremendously uncomfortable due to the fact that your emotions and feelings will arise, join the club. But this is what makes actively listening so essential when you're on your journey to Self.

As someone is talking to you, tune-in very closely not only to what they are saying but also how you are feeling. If you have something to say, say it in your head or write it down in your phone but do not lose focus on the fact that you are actively listening but remain silent. Staying silent allows you to feel in places you thought you wouldn't know you had in the first place. After having a conversation and you have free time to journal, do that, whether it's on your phone or in an actual journal or you can even talk to yourself on the way home from that person's house. Ask yourself how you felt while you were listening, things you wanted to say in the conversation and why, and also if you did say anything (hypothetically) ask yourself would it have helped the conversation or not. You would be in awe of what you will discover about yourself.

For example, when I began to actively listen to people, I realized I had a feeling of ALWAYS wanting to say something more than purely listening (also known as a BAD listener of course). But what I really learned about myself was that, restraining myself caused anger, frustration, and I literally felt like I was choking. Later I found that this was because I always wanted to be heard. I realized I never had the capacity of hearing others and I did not like that about myself. It was a frustrating discovery due to the fact that I always want to help people, but the only way to help people is to listen to what they need help with, so I welcomed this uncomfortable epiphany. I began to see why people didn't like talking to me about things...I found this out through the list of things I wanted to say that I later wrote down in my journal after a conversation I had with someone. The amount of facts and things I learned from a book that I just wanted to share had nothing to do with the conversation at all. I realized by reflecting on the "conversation" I had with people by actively just listening, majority of the time none of the things I have learned or had facts on wasn't even needed to be said. I also noticed when I did slightly speak, although the challenge was not to speak, the few things I had to say came from an area that was pure and my truth and obviously needed to surface itself regardless of the exercise. I noticed the feeling I had when this happened, it felt GREAT, it felt needed, it felt received! It created moments in the conversation that made the person either feel heard or got them thinking deeper than they expected.

Actively listening will help you find out what kind of person you already are, whether you like this person or discover you do not, and it will help you find out what person you rather be. More simple self-discoveries but necessary.

In the Silence

Just be quiet. Literally.

For some, this is easy and for others, this is hard. Especially now that you are addicted to talking to yourself. Plot TWIST! Do not confuse this with the listening practice mentioned above.

Silence is equally important to the conversations you have with yourself on your daily commute. In silence, within this journey you will begin to feel the now married mind and soul as ONE. This is completeness, like no other. To get away from the poetic hoopla, let me say this as well... within silence (separate from meditation) you will feel the balance or what I like to call, the homeostasis of what it brings to your life. Your actual body lives to always create balance; if your sugar level is too high, there are things in the body that will activate to level it out, if you are hot... your body activates the sweat glands. Actively practicing silence will give you a measure of what peace may feel like through its own created homeostasis throughout this journey.

We all know how to be exhausted or let's say...feel exhausted, we thrive on this feeling because if we don't feel it, we will question if we did anything at all! The best way to start practicing silence is after doing one of the practices, using one of the tools, or methods mentioned in this book. I say "after", because you already gave yourself something to do and now you will feel "worthy" of a break. In this silence just let your mind be still...that's it! Say nothing and just do whatever you are doing. Yes, your mind may respond to something, so let it but don't outwardly respond. That shortness of the feeling of peace will become a craving, and so every time you sway out of it you will begin to want to go back to it, which again I say, will create this homeostasis within the married soul and the mind.

Now, meditation is a practice that brings the consciousness to what peace may feel like as the divine beings that we are and the practice of silence may lead you to the same. But I believe the difference is that silence is creating a place where the soul and mind, in a relationship, finds balance in their coexistence during this lifetime of BEING. Whereas meditation is the divine feeling of peace that being in silence can help oneself measure when we are imbalanced. Silence is just quick and easy to lead into meditation, but even if you never pick up the practice of meditation you have learned the simple act of silence.

"The must needed exhale of BEING is silence." -tif

Relationships

Although I agree that loving yourself is important before you really know how to love someone else, I do believe you can also learn self-love through loving on someone or them loving on you. You don't have to understand yourself fully nor do you have to understand what love is before being in a relationship. But you still have to have self-love for a relationship to succeed. Within relationships you will always be discovering what love "is" (for you) whether it's for yourself, for another person or as a combination of two people trying their best to coexist.

You'll be surprised what relationships bring into your life whether there are tools on how to love someone better.... like books, tests, counseling or even conversations with others. All of these will provoke something within to dive deeper into resources of finding things out for yourself.

Simply being in a relationship of any kind, even platonic will help you discover a lot about yourself and love. There is no escaping no matter how many "failed" relationships you have, you will ALWAYS discover something. Do not allow the hardening of your heart deprive you from what was needed to be learned from the experience. If relationships are something you find yourself in or wanting, allow it to show you things on the daily by just being present. As things arise and surfaces, allow both your heart and mind to journey through it and there you will find the soul guiding you if you are to listen to it.

Working/Chores

Being in a state of unconscious habit is the worst thing you can do to yourself but it's inevitable. But adding these small miniscule conscious habits that I'm about to mention, into the big habits of daily life will probably give the word, standing alone, a better outlook. This practice is applying the now created homeostasis through silence with your daily life of chores and work life or just the daily mundane.

Sitting at a computer or phone and looking at your bank account is something we do in a moment, whether it's after spending some money or starting your day off by looking at how much money you have in your account. In that same moment of looking, whether it starts from typing in your password or user name, acknowledge whatever feelings or reaction that comes up, whether you close one eye or hold your breath before the next screen comes up or you get excited. Simply acknowledging those feelings will allow you to see yourself and probably help you figure out ways to avoid those feelings later. You will probably begin thinking of ways on how you can acquire joy instead of the anxiousness you discovered during this small exercise. Ask yourself why do I close an eye? Is it because I spend too much money? Is it because I hate annual fees?

Or is it because the amount in there never changes? Or you have too many unwanted bills? When asking yourself that, exhale, and then let it go. Proceed at looking in your account do whatever you had to do or wanted to do. But before putting down your phone or computer look around your environment and assess your feelings as well, THEN go ahead and go about your day. Do this over and over again. Within doing this small thing every time, you will most likely unconsciously make changes to avoid the bad feelings or increase the good feelings.

For example, if opening that app to your bank account makes you anxious and uncomfortable, simply by acknowledging those feelings over time you will begin to try to avoid those feelings by making changes. These changes may look like; if it's about overspending money and always seeing a negative amount in your bank you may begin to stop spending money on things you may not need. If it's about unwanted bills you may change your phone services to something that is cheaper, if it's about the amount never changing you may begin to pick up side jobs or investing. Your mind and soul are beautiful mechanisms that will put you into action if you allow yourself to be more conscious of things including small emotions and feelings in your daily life. This can work with positive emotions as well. If you're always excited to see that your paycheck has been deposited, you would eventually begin to want to have more excitement so you may find other revenues from acquiring more money. Also, if you begin to notice that you are no longer excited you will in-turn, do the same thing of finding other revenues as well to regain that excitement you once felt.

You may even discover your relationship with money whether good or bad. You might find out that you need control and discipline or you will find out that you're really good at budgeting. You may also realize things are not for you or you have a passion to help others with their accounts. This activity/practice of assessing your feelings and actions in your daily life can be applied to anything, like doing chores out of habit. You may discover you hate going home because you have a lot to do when it comes to chores. Just acknowledging that feeling of not wanting to go home, you may change the way you do your morning routine. Instead of throwing clothes around in a rush to get to work you may want to wake up earlier or set out some clothes prior to the morning. I can go on and on about daily routines and assessing feelings that will lead you to discovering change in self-discovery but we must proceed onto other topics.

Applying the method/practice of; silence = Creating Homeostasis with the married mind and soul + daily life chores $-/+$ the negative/ positive feelings= momentum/ change/ACTION.

The beautiful thing about all of this is that, by one simple and small thing like assessing a feeling once and awhile will create change, and help you acknowledge things about yourself without "REAL WORK!"

Random Pauses

This topic is similar to the above topics but what I am about to describe here will lead into something that may help you understand meditation a little more than how it is usually advertised in the media. What I am talking about is; the silent monk on a hill, eyes closed, legs pretzeled, hands on the knees and quiet and still for hours. I bring this up because I have ran into a lot of people including my own mother saying that they cannot meditate even though they were told that meditation isn't really silence of the mind for hours/minutes, especially when you first start. Let's see if I can make this less tasking and small to swallow....

Begin with putting down your phone for two deep breaths, then pick it up again. You're done.

Okay, during a commercial while watching tv, turn off your television or pause it and take three deep breaths with your eyes closed, then un-pause or turn it back on. You're Done.

Before bed and after watching a bunch of reels, notice your hands and feet and then scan over your entire body, watch your eyes close and let your thoughts tire you out. Include deep breaths. There, you're done.

Whilst listening to someone talk, take three deep breaths...then continue to just listen. All Done.

Do any of these things repeatedly and as often as possible. But I would like you to add to the count of breaths you take every time you do any of these things.

You will probably begin to think how silly it is or start

thinking about your show you were just watching or even how the hell reading this book got you doing this exercise...let your thoughts roam. The beautiful thing about breathing is that you have to exhale after an inhale and vice versa. There's a quick pause in between, even in the slightest. Same thing applies to thoughts...eventually there will be a pause, a silence. Within this practice you will find this truth. This is what meditation looks like even in the smallest form.

When you sit and actually take out time to try to meditate you do not instantly become like the monk on a mountain. Your legs and butt will hurt, you will slouch and have no idea on what to do with your hands. Most importantly, you will have so many thoughts. Ha! Silence? Peace? Umm yeah.... NO. But that's okay, that's normal! Let your thoughts go. Eventually you would need a mental exhale and BOOM you hear the birds outside your window even if it was for a second and then your thoughts reappear. Keep going until your leg hurts or your butt can't take it anymore.

Meditation will be an entire practice that will be something that will "take" out time in your day. Sorry-not-sorry. To connect with the higher self, it takes time in relationship with it. Just like you would do with God/ the Divine/ the Creator. You cannot go into a journey thinking that eventually you would need to take some time out to tap into the relationship of SELF...but we will talk about that later, maybe in another book. For now, we aren't here to talk about taking time out, we are talking about it being a part of your time of daily life, so do the small moments of conscious breath with the remote in your hand. It'll gift you something on your journey, I promise. Even if it's just the annoyance of you even trying it. I thank you in advance for trying.

Exploring New Areas

Imagine you have a Unicorn Day, meaning no work, no kids, no more chores....and you decide to go to your local mall or Barnes and Noble to indulge in some time alone... and then you go home. Then on another Unicorn Day, you do it again. And then you eventually make it a habit. On an entirely different day, maybe while driving to work in another area you see a mall and think "Hmm...that's a big mall, one day I should go look". Well, another Unicorn Day comes around and instead of going to your local areas you usually go to; you decide to go into the mall that's on your usual commute towards work instead. There you find that this mall carries stores you only saw in movies, there's a fancy carousel, and people to help you in every bathroom, and a sitting area with televisions and a BARNES AND NOBLE WITH THREE STORIES! (Yes, this happened to me). You spend your Unicorn Day there, and then go home...well now you begin to want that experience again. You begin to sift through the emotions and feelings you had while being there and then realize that's the lifestyle you want.

I gave this as an example to say this, when exploring different places even if it is the "same" type of places you usually go but in a different area, it may spark a part of you that you never knew about prior. We sometimes get so content in our daily lives and our daily status of just being where we are, we don't get the opportunity to see, literally where we long to be. We all have dreamed of our future but we rarely allow ourselves to sample it. This is a way of sampling what we want for ourselves even if you haven't yet discovered what you may want your future to look like. Of course, we dream of our careers, cars, homes, and luxury vacations but never the simple environment that surrounds those things, like the mall, bookstore, gas station, or even community. We think we need money to travel across the world to grow experiences, when in all actuality it's just around the corner or on your daily commute.

You never know what you REALLY want until you feel the joy of your soul move beyond the emotions and feelings you are used to encountering.

Vision Boarding

I will be honest, I never enjoyed vision boards. The magazine type ones I mean. For some reason destroying any type of book hurts me... although I am guilty of destroying a book for art pieces. I don't want to talk about it though, it was a rough moment for me. Not only are we destroying some sort of book, I disliked doing vision boards because it felt too restricted and boxed in. Like, once I put these things on this board, I must aim for exactly that, and if I don't, I fail. Although I dislike vision boards, I find it useful for one's journey to self by putting your vision onto something you can see every day. But what I suggest you use, is a platform that is easier to access and create on the go like Pinterest.

When I found out what Pinterest was, I was actually delighted. I was happy to partake in this social media platform because with this app I had many more options and I could change and rearrange the items I saved if I wanted to. Oh, the power in the delete button is like ecstasy for me.

Pinterest is a "visual discovery engine" according to the help section of the app, it is a place that can inspire you through its wide selections of pins like; recipes, interior design ideas and areas to travel. It is an app that provides you an organized way of saving things you like.

Vision boarding through this app or any app that is similar will help you acknowledge your likes; past, present, and future by looking at what you constantly click on and what you saved. Simply doing this, you are reintroducing yourself to Self every time you log on and browse through your PINNED items. When you focus your time on this app you can begin to create sections within all of your saved pins to form a vision board. For example, you can create a saved section that focuses on what your dream home will be. Yes, you can do the same thing with actual vision boarding that consists of paper being glued on a poster board, but I love the app because you can find a lot more options and with that, a lot of different dream homes. Through this you may begin to find out that you really didn't want a five-bedroom house but instead three beds would be okay as long as it's by the beach with a dock nearby or as long as it has a big kitchen. It is a funny thing how your brain can be so set on one thing but when it is presented with multiple possibilities you begin to change and actually feel different about what your wants may be.

Not only having these types of apps is a great way of getting more options and exploring yourself in a deeper way through the multiple selections, but it also doesn't take time out of your day. You can simply be at your desk, on a break, scrolling through Pinterest and save a pin in an instant. And later, maybe out of boredom, organize all that has been saved while watching TV.

By no means am I advertising for Pinterest or saying "Everyone should get it!" What I am trying to get at here, is that we can use already existing platforms made to enjoy on our devices to allow the soul to journey with us on the surface. I am a scrap artist, so I tend to see beauty in using already made things into other things, upcycling. Well, I have this same skill with things we use on a daily basis that can provide spaces where we can allow our soul to come into union in our daily lives instead of just on Sundays or when we finally realize we have one when we cry. We realize life is short... We owe it to ourselves to be what we are made to be, a Soul living a bodied experience. It's about time we know how, and use everything we already have to do so.

CHAPTER SEVEN

Upcycling, Meeting where we are

In a society that loves finding the easiest ways of doing things, I have found a way to do some of this SELF-Journey work by simply upcycling the tools we already have and not interrupting your day-to-day lifestyle, because god- forbid we add more actual conscious work when the unconscious way of living has been here for centuries.

With all snarky tone aside, I truly have realized the ruling of unconsciousness. I too, am guilty of finding ways to incorporate work on self without actually working. Although I am one of the few that enjoys diving deep every day, laziness is a huge part of our lifestyle and I have come to terms with that. So here we are, a society that notices that we are lazy, notices we are numb to the soul and know we need change. But some of us want to just throw the whole world into the trash and start all over. "I'm waiting for Jesus' return" is a religious way of laziness by the way... "We must destroy the partocracy!" is just a destruction of the old but building anew on confusion if the soul hasn't been in use for centuries. "So tif, what do we do?" You ask. Honestly, I don't know exactly, but that doesn't mean I don't have an answer.

We have been using a tool that keeps us "connected" to one another on the daily to a point that we are basically glued to it! Yes, I am talking about our phones. On our phones we use social media to connect to the world more than anything. On these platforms we connect to family, friends, work, school and communities we create or want to be a part of. More than ever, now because of covid. But really, we had this addiction prior to the VID.

We use social media as a platform to advocate our beliefs of all kinds, to find connection and ultimately, whether we are conscious of it or not, OUR PURPOSE. Majority of the time we are looking for a reason. A reason to feel, a reason to be, a reason to live, a reason through connection...over-all we are on our phones 99% of the time and that 1%, we are sleep for four hours at the most (an extreme over exaggeration for dramatic effects although this is true for many of us). We are mindlessly scrolling for hours on hours. But what if we can set up this tool of connection to also consciously connect with ourselves, our soul?

Platforms, the stage already Exist

Instagram is my favorite social media platform. And if it is yours as well then you will probably adopt this method of upcycling this tool by using it as a way to connect to self on the daily, if you haven't already. For those who have an Instagram but are barely on it because it doesn't resonate or you hate how lost and/or vulnerable it leaves you, maybe you will find some peace after hearing what I have to say. Lastly, for those who don't have one yet, I hope when or if you do get one you will use this "method" when you start.

Honestly Instagram needs some updating in many areas on its platform and maybe by the time you read this, they have. So, this is for the basic encounters with the app. We're not talking about how it can be updated, but instead upcycled as the platform that it already is. Before we dive into this upcycle method let's start here, my first suggestion is to simply POST. Post whatever you like, with whatever caption that feels right to you or no caption at all. Many people hesitate to post things for many reasons, but the one I hear the most is that they would regret having posted a post later. Don't be caught up on that, there's a reason for the **delete** button but I suggest using the archive selection. Archive your photos, this is coming from a person who finds the ultimate pleasure in the delete button, but I do highly suggest you use the **archive** button instead. Even if you post it and in that same moment you archive it. Just begin to post! Remember this is YOUR PAGE, not the World's.

Posting instead of overthinking about whether if you'll like it, regret it, or if you'll get a lot of likes has a positive effect, it is the beginning of being vulnerable to yourself, although it leaves you open to your followers (don't think too much into that right now). If any type of vulnerability makes you feel too uncomfortable, ARCHIVE it and come to it later to see if you really want to have it on your page. The beauty of this button is, in your Archive section you will see how your page will be set up before you even actually post it on your page. With having your post ARCHIVED immediately, you get to see the arrangement before releasing them onto your page, which happens to be another reason people tend to not post pics, or wait a long period of time until they decide on how they want their page to look like.

We have all come across very creative ways of how you can set up your Instagram profiles. And even if we find one that we like, and finally decide to create our page just like it, we then see another page with a different setup and now want to have our page looking like that. Unfortunately, we do not have the rearrange button for some reason, (unless you get a separate app to assist you) so we are left with all these already LIKED pictures and now either have the option to DELETE/ARCHIVE and set up the next batch of post like how we want it now. STOP. It is okay to add a few filler posts instead of deleting or archiving already liked pics. Filler posts are what I define as either blank white or colored posts or actual pics of a bunch of back-to-back grass pics or any scenery of your selection. These types of posts are unspoken indicators of change on your account although many people will be confused on why there are a bunch of white photos being on their feed. So now we have an option that leaves us with our prior already like pics and now we have new posts being arranged the way we like it. Funny how small freedoms make you feel good. Or this is utterly ridiculous and you are wondering why I put so much thought into this. Well, I will explain later... moving on!

Secondly, after getting used to posting whatever you like and probably archiving them immediately until you are ready. Make sure to get a profile picture and bio that fits you in the moment, if you haven't already, and if you have, look at it now! If not satisfied, change it. Although many people struggle with the actual posting on their account, I haven't run across anyone struggling with the choice of posting a profile pic. For some reason a lot of people don't really overthink about deleting and changing their profile pic. Maybe it's because they won't lose likes or receive likes on it. Now for the bio, a lot of people feel more liberated in changing and updating it.

Okay here, we are...hopefully in a spot of power over our own account...although we didn't do much so far.
Unfortunately, Instagram and other social media platforms tend to have so much power over us to a point we don't really realize it. Earlier I mentioned that you may be curious as to why I have put so much thought into this subject, well it's because over the years I have run into SO MANY individuals who had these odd, random struggles with social media platforms, specifically Instagram. I noticed this only because that was my go-to platform of communication for so many reasons. Once I got them to meet

me on there, I would ask why they had little to no post or even ask why they were so hesitant to using this method of communication. Some of the reasons, if not most of them, were because they did not know what or how they wanted to go about posting. It's crazy how these platforms cause an identity crisis within the most confident individuals. It really makes some people think so deeply on how they want to present themselves and sometimes no matter how they do, the receivers of that presentation will judge it. I mean, it's okay and you may be unbothered by the lack of likes or comments, but the over exposure of yourself will cause some extreme uncomfortability. If you're anything like me, you are forever changing, jumping in and out of boxes. Boxes that are desperately trying its best to fit people into a short description for the sake of others. This two-dimensional platform could never keep up with a forever growing 3-dimensional being, but here we are on the daily trying to fit everything that we are and want to be on it regardless!

We are already trapped guys! We are already in the habit of being on it, so let's work with our captors, because we have proven ourselves as human beings, that we can evolve under any conditions.

Just like how in chapter six I have shown some ways of surfacing the soul in our daily lives by embedding soul work into your daily activities, we can also do it here.

Reclaiming Your profile
We already talked about posting, deleting,

and archiving...this is all part of reclaiming your profile. I would like to stress that LIKES are not important! Authenticity is, and through that, I truly believe LIKES will follow. And if they don't, at least you still have your sanity and a loud SIGN that screams that being Instagram famous is not your calling, YET. So, reclaim your energy of social media by creating for yourself! What do you want to post? What do you want to see every time you log in? Do you want your account to be private or public for the time being? Do you know, even if you are public, you can block followers? It may require a little more attentiveness but you have the power on who sees what. Hide your story from people, choose to post for your friends only by using the CLOSE FRIENDS option. There you go. Just reclaim your Account.

Stalking yourself

To add upon the hours of scrolling, we don't only lose time but also, we tend to lose ourselves by comparing ourselves to others. We are constantly comparing our looks and life to others. We stay on other people's pages longer than our own. STOP that! Like I mentioned before within this book, the feeling of inadequacy is a curse and sometimes we are the ones cursing ourselves the most. It's okay to look at other people's pages but make sure to STALK your page more than you do others (please stop stalking people actually). An easy way in doing this is simply to rely on when you begin to have a coveting feeling. Meaning, the moment you begin to feel sad, angry, jealous or low because you "wish this or that" when looking at something on Instagram, instantly go to your page and scroll through it. If you feel any of these low feelings, ask yourself what is missing from your page? Then ask what are some small changes or additives you can make to your page more appealing to you, aka STALK WORTHY.

If that doesn't work, you can do another method by simply going to your page every time someone follows you and look at it as if you are that person. It may be a bit much, but try and see if that works. It really makes you think about if you really care about what other people think of your page or not. With knowing that, you can solidify your true wants and what you really care about on your page versus what you are doing for others or likes. Getting closer to a genuine YOU is the purpose here. You can also create another page to look within yours. This will bring you all the way out and into the observer seats. The mind is a fascinating thing when it works with the soul on this journey of self. Sometimes you have to do something weird to discover what works for you.

By no means am I condoning STALKING of others!

Soul Algorithm

We all know what an algorithm is and if not,

Definition;

An Algorithm is
a process or set of rules to be followed in calculations or other problem-solving operations, especially by a computer.

Within the topic of social media, an algorithm is a way social media platforms use what you, the user, clicks on the most while on the app and feeds you more posts and/or advertisements like it. For example, if the user while scrolling, always click on funny memes, after a period of time, the app will begin to give the user more selections of funny memes and maybe start having pop up ads that are funny and/or pop up of clothing that has memes printed on it for the user to buy. So, it is not just a coincidence that you are always seeing funny memes every time you log on. Many of us would deem these coincidences as signs from above, especially those who are always looking for topics on love and divinity. Sorry to burst your bubble, but it's not a sign. But it is a great way of showing you that you have more control of what you want to see and maybe, need to see. Let's make this algorithm work for our soul, shall we?

Since we have more control on what we see on this platform than we thought (minus the hidden agenda working itself into our lives at certain times), let's create a space where we can stay conscious of our soul, whatever that may be. Start with clicking on things and following pages that resonate with you now and what you want to see for yourself in the future. I personally, began to click and follow anything that had modern homes, pit bulls, Divine femininity, Divine Masculinity, crystals, Jeeps, black cats, cats, health, mental health, and beautiful places. How do you do this? Go to search, type in what you are looking for and press the hashtag option and BOOM, begin to follow whatever resonates. After doing that, you will see these things pop up often enough and that's when you begin to like, save, share and/or comment. Afterwhile the algorithm to your account will begin to change.

Constantly seeing the things you resonate with and want to see in your future will not ONLY make you more conscious of your soul, it will also do a magical thing that we call manifestation. But let me not throw the magical rainbow glitter yet.

Instagram isn't the only platform that can be upcycled. Selecting anything that you do or use on a daily basis can be a tool to bring the soul to the surface. This may seem a bit "much" but WHY NOT? Why not just do it? You are already on your phone 95% of the time. On this journey of self-exploration, growth, love and overall, our purpose, we should see the importance of bringing soul consciousness to our lives. We have left so much to the mind and body... it's unfortunate but now it's the perfect time for us to finally put in efforts to be an entire BEING, purposeful and full of unexplained magic.

CHAPTER EIGHT

The Present of Gratitude

Through this entire journey of self, you will find out that all the cliché quotes about self-love, growth and purpose are true. Yup, I wrote an entire book that really could have just been a whole day of scrolling hashtags or Googling on the topic, but here we are.

I do want to give you your money's worth, so I will emphasize some cliché sayings that should be taken to heart; "Be Present" and anything /everything that is on the lines of "Always be grateful". If you walk away from this book learning anything let it be that. Acknowledging and finding self, and allowing the soul to be a big part of your life causes the immense feeling of gratefulness. There's no avoiding that, after this journey or even during the journey. It is true that you begin to overflow with this love and with that overflow I suggest you put it into gratitude. Honestly each time you wake up in the morning, name five things that you're grateful for. Or pause randomly throughout the day and list a few things. It's something about gratitude that just wraps every piece of self-work done on this journey into a nice present for the rest of your life.

Along the side of being grateful, is being present. With the action of naming a few things you are grateful for; you cannot avoid being present. Simply because you have to literally name things you "have" at the moment to conjure a list.

Being present comes with a gift of more GIFTS. What I mean by this is...you know the saying "God doesn't give you more than what you can bear?" (If you don't... it is kind of self-explanatory) well, with this saying I want you to acknowledge that it also means, He (she, the divine) will not give you more things than what you already have if you are not grateful for them.

I love using what I have learned by being a parent to see how maybe our Creator continues to raise us. Being a mother of young toddlers, I begin to spoil them with whatever toy they want. But I soon realize how quickly they toss these same exact toys to the side within hours of getting them. So, I stopped getting them toys, but of course my family continued. My heart began to get heavy time after time watching these little blessed beings be given everything they want, to only see it broken within hours. I then started to tell them that they will no longer get any new toys until I see them taking care of their present ones. Now knowing that, they begin to play with every toy and with time, they grew a pleasant attachment to them and saw their toys with so much value, that I now have the urge to run back to go get them if they were left at a place, like a store we were just at. Watching my kids value the things they had, not only made me want to buy them anything they want again, but they also began to ask for things to add to the present toy that they already had or an upgrade of the same thing, which I was so willing to buy them with no hesitation. You probably see where I'm going. Right?

Being grateful for the things, not only gives you the gift of present-ness but also more GIFTS! Even if you don't believe in God, you will soon find out that we block ourselves from our own wants by feeling unworthy. This unworthiness can stem from the subconscious mind where we acknowledge that we do not deserve something because we don't take care of ourselves or the things we already have. We may want a bigger house but day in and day out we allow the house we have to fall apart. Our mind may be in cahoots of being like a parent to an ungrateful child. Like I said before, it's amazing how the mind works with the soul. And for those who can just buy new things, have you ever wondered why you feel empty inside once you have it?

Gratitude leads to present-ness (and vice versa by the way) ...present-ness leads to valuing the things you have and like magic, cue the Rainbow Glitter, gifts of manifestations come into reality. Who would have imagined that being curious about your very existence can lead you to a place of such riches.

MEANINGFULL

CHAPTER NINE

MANIFESTATION-ING

Here we are, at a place where you never thought this book would lead to. And to be completely honest, neither did I. My entire goal was to simply suggest that many of you begin to start your journey of finding yourself, your purpose and acknowledge the need to live a soul conscious life. It wasn't until now that this topic hit me. All this work naturally leads you to this method of extreme movement, which makes sense since we are co-creators. We were born to create... an innate power we tend to ignore. Some of us understand our "need" to procreate, some of us can't live without creating some sort of piece of art and others find jobs and hobbies that keep their hands moving, a NEED. But when it comes to creating a "greater" life than what has been given, we tend to settle. "Too bad" that this journey creates a key to unlock such a gift...I hope it is really hard to ignore.

Definition:

MANIFEST

(verb); to make evident or certain by showing or displaying

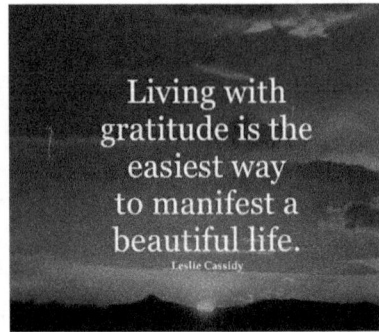

The practice that is Manifestation, became very mainstream as of late. Although it's been here for centuries it is being more adopted and less taboo. Unfortunately I see a pattern, maybe it's because I come from a Christian background, that if the Churches began to adopt these practices, a lot of things that once were taboo are no longer. Nonetheless I am grateful that it's getting into homes and people's lifestyles. The practice of manifesting comes from a lot of other cultures and religions. You may hear it be called, Law of Attraction as well.

When I first came across this practice I thought of it as another method of Escapism, being a Pisces and working on my shadow self that includes this toxic trait of Escapism

124

and daydreaming all day. It really put fear into me at the time. I thought this was another form of Escapism that will consume me after all this work I have done on my journey. So, I ignored it until I realized later on my journey, there is no escaping such a power once soul work has been done. Even if you read about the law of attraction (the more Scientific form of manifesting), it talks about starting within to create a desired external experience/outcome. Whatever occurs within self will always create an outer experience whether it's bad or good. For example, if you're always wallowing in depression and pessimism, then your life will reflect such energy. There is no way you cannot believe that, because we all have experienced such things at one point of our lives. Thank God there is some scientific proof of this that we can find with ease so it no longer sounds like some magical hoopla. Please find out for yourself, do some research and honestly, it might not take much to find these answers due to its popularity. I am not here to walk you through it because you must experience it and have a belief system that will allow it to be your truth. I am here to give you ways of how to tap into it without feeling like you're taking too much time out of your daily life, because "God forbid, we make work look like work!"

I would suggest you apply these practices after you have done some of the practices and methods mentioned above first. Find who you are, discover self-love, find what works for you and your soul so you "two" finally connect (body and soul). When you begin this side of the journey, I am hoping that you will see the "light" of what manifestation really is with much more ease than just reading this chapter. Also, it doesn't really work like magic as it may come off to be described as (although will often call it as such). Ultimately manifesting doesn't really "work" without gratitude and present-ness.

Let's talk about ways you can manifest without much "work".

It all begins with a vision so begin to vision board, dream, and think of places you want to go. We already talked about using our phones and apps that we use on the daily to help us unite soul with reality. So once again let's go to Instagram. While using Instagram you can set it up in ways to mimic your vision. Once you have a vision of what you would like in the near future or far future, begin to create your page to mimic that. Whether you actually start going to places that have the quality of life you want and snap pictures of you there, or finding pictures from google (be careful of copyrights) and posting them on your story or on your account. It's kind of like fake it until you make it. But I do warn you not to project a false lifestyle. I know that this sounds contradicting but to avoid creating a false lifestyle, just add in your captions; #manifestit or something on the lines that says, "One day I'll be here," or, "Coming soon." Or simply post unapologetically and if anybody is curious, they will ask you. Be honest with yourself about your present reality while reaching or creating a life you will end up with.

Another way you can use a vision board on this app is, use your saved post section. Instagram gives you an option to save other accounts' posts. And provides you a section where you can go see what you have saved, you can organize it to your liking. This is similar to Pinterest which is another app you can use for your daily visual boarding which has been already mentioned. The reason why I say to do this, is because it begins to allow your brain and reality AND your soul to work as one to always see where you're heading. Putting things that you want in the future in the present time as if you already have it or worthy of it will allow manifestations to come much quicker. And I hate to say much quicker because it's not like it's an instant. I am one of the believers that believe that time has no concept, but unfortunately, we live in a society that base life on a made-up system of time (but I won't get into that right now). So, what I mean by, "it will manifest quickly", is that you will be so caught up in self work, being grateful in the present and combining manifesting into your daily life that when you begin to look up and see the major changes you will be surprised how quickly they came.

Another small way you can use your phone by putting the vision in your hands, is by changing your lock screen and home screen on your device to the thing or things you are aiming for. Boom, simple. Drown yourself in the vision!

Now let's get a little bit crazier, but crazy fun. As children we always played pretend. It was inevitable that we were going to grow up and have a job or become a parent and probably do A LOT of chores. Back then it was fun, now reality has sat in and it's probably not as much fun. But

127

let's use this method of playing pretend. I honestly stress that you first visit places like I've mentioned in chapter 6 before playing Adult Pretend. I suggest this because, of course pictures and our brain are capable of putting us in those places we've never been but it's different when you actually have been to the places. I'm not saying travel the world and then do this, you may not have the finances for that. I am simply reiterating what I said in chapter 6 about you going to areas that mimic the lifestyle you want. After doing this, while you are home or in your local area you can apply this game of pretend, it will allow you to not only see the places you want to be in in the future, but you will also feel the experience again after you went to that place; the smells, the noises...the sensory factory will vibrate so high.

Now that you see where I'm going with this, let's apply this method. When you are at the mall, begin to imagine that mall as the mall you went to in a different area on that Unicorn Day and watch your posture change, and the feelings within yourself change. Close your eyes for a brief second and wake up to that mall while you're in your local mall. Do the same thing at your local gas station, we all have experienced the random gas station that was fancier than the one we usually go to, so envision that exact gas station as you pump your gas into your car. Let's take it further by imagining your present car being the car of your dreams. Try it before you knock it, once the brain begins to constantly drown your senses with the things you want in life, you'll be amazed how your body will begin to move to obtain those exact things. And at this point it's not tricking the mind, it is literally your soul putting everything into the world to give you what you believe you are worthy of.

The beautiful thing about this method is that you will begin to get accustomed to it. Life has so many ups and downs and changes, so it's inevitable that your vision or visions begin to change slightly here and there. Whether it's because you have met someone new (like a romantic partner) who has a slightly different vision for the future and you're genuinely open to morphing your vision just slightly to fit theirs, or you experience something different and now your dream home is slightly skewed to another version. I am here to say that's OK, it doesn't mess up the "magic" of manifestation. These changes will help you sift through feelings, emotions and really test your flexibility on a subject.

If you run across something that changes your vision that you already started manifesting, whether it's a new experience or person that came into your life, like a romantic partner, try playing adult pretend.

For example, one day I was very infatuated with a man that I was spending a lot of time with and he considered a future with me as well, but during our talks our visions of our house or one of our houses was different then I wanted the house to be. It made me uncomfortable because for me, the type of home I want is a priority above most things that I vision for my future. So, using the method of "Adult Pretend" while I was showering, I envisioned myself in the home I have already envisioned over and over again. I began talking to this man in my head that I was interested in at the present time as if he was only six feet away from where I was showering. I began a conversation in my head but carried it out loud, as well, again while I was showering. I envisioned that I was in my future bathroom of the home, I analyzed my feelings on how the conversation was going and how he would probably respond and after that I assessed if I was OK with him being a part of my life. Then asked myself if I was okay if that home looked different. The conversation was an experience that allowed me to see that I liked him more than I thought and with that conclusion, I was OK if my upcoming house changed. I also realized the possibilities of still receiving my dream house and later upgrading to a different home after "we" have lived an amount of time in that house. After that, of course when I saw him, by divine alignment he mentioned the same possibility without me having to say anything about my shower experience. Do you see where I'm going with this?

I love this method because it's a constant check-in with yourself. You don't always have to see if your vision works with other people. You can play this type of adult pretend by just simply talking to yourself randomly. I know I talk about talking to yourself a lot but it's a beautiful practice to adopt. No matter how crazy it may look. It gives you a type of freedom, in a beautiful connection to Self. Yes, we can journal, that is another option. But I honestly and truly want us to start talking out loud to ourselves.

Let's begin to create more passionately through our lives

with all the innate tools we were made of. You can call it magic; we can call it a superpower; we can call ourselves gods. All I know is that there is so much proof in the pudding and we need to stop ignoring it.

CHAPTER TEN

JOURNEYED & Beyond

Purpose

Definition; (NOUN)

1. a subject under discussion or an action in course of execution

(VERB)

2. to purpose as an aim to oneself

Self

Definition; (NOUN)

1. the union of elements (such as body, emotions, thoughts, and sensations) that constitute the individuality and identity of a person

Soul

MEANINGFULL

Definition; (NOUN)

1. a person's total self

Journey

Definition; (NOUN)

1. something suggesting travel or passage from one place to another
2. an act or instance of traveling from one place to another

We started acknowledging we are made of Love and reached into the stars, then stretched ourselves towards the ground so our souls will feel the dirt beneath its toes. Now we're here, just at the end of this book but hopefully this is just the beginning of your journey.

Don't think too far into the tools and methods and practices we went over. All the hoopla that made you uncomfortable, is in all actuality a great indicator of change. Natal charts don't have to be your thing, remember there are so many tools out there about learning about self no matter how the question is formed. Whether it's, What is my purpose? Why am I here? What am I supposed to be doing with my life? Just know that love is the answer no matter how cliche that may sound. Although we have 10,000 definitions of what love is and what it looks like, know that love is action. So, it only makes sense if you learn what love is through actual methods of DOING. Maybe a relationship will show you what love is, maybe it's simply being the crazy person sitting in the theater by yourself laughing and enjoying your time.

Don't let anything stop you. Not even your lowest days. Even within your lows, you will find some sort of practice, method or even hobby that will show you more about yourself. So go out there and adopt a plant. No matter what it is, have peace in knowing that whoever created us ensured that we will have everything we need to answer any questions we have. Especially about ourselves.

Through your journey of learning yourself and using whatever works for you, we know the next level is inevitable. Our journey will send us to a place where we acknowledge that our soul is a huge part of our lives, if not, our lives in general. Our purpose is simply Being. Once we understand that, it is beautiful how gifts are innately unlocked and remind us that we are Co-creators. Maybe that is simply our purpose, to be what we were made to be, Creators.

Who knew that this book will lead us to a place greater than just an "answer" which is within your ENTIRE JOURNEY whatever the answer you find it to be. I want to believe that this journey will bring us all to a place of power individually and whatever that does for us collectively is to be announced. One journey at a time and then, BEYOND.

NOTES

Chapter One: All we need is LOVE

"Love." *Merriam-Webster.com Dictionary*, Merriam-Webster, https://www.merriam-webster.com/dictionary/love. Accessed 2 Oct. 2021.

"*Love you your life...*"meme. 55 funny love Memes to share with that special Someone, WinkGo March 13, 2017, https//: winkgo.com

"Meaningful." *Merriam-Webster.com Dictionary, Merriam-Web ster, https://www.merriam-webster.com/dictionary/meaning ful. Accessed (Sept.29, 2021).*

"*My love and affection...*" meme. 28 memes about Relationships, Bar norma.com, oct.20,2011, https//: banorma.com/relationships

"*The day I met you*" meme. 20mcheesy and amusingly funny memes, wordsporn, November 22, 2016, https//:wordsporn. com/20cheesyandamusinglyfunnymemesforyour-husband

"*The first time...*" meme. Lost love memes, mememonkey.com, Janu ary 12,2017,https//:memesmonkey.com/lostlovememes

Chapter Two: Natal Charts, the Hoopla

JD Miller- one of the most driven individuals I met in 2020. Entre-preneur.

Charts

The Twelve Houses of Astrology. Adapted from "What Houses In Your Birth Chart Mean and How to Find Them" by A. K. Fara gher, June 8 2021, Allure Online. Retrieved Sept. 28, 2021, from https://www.allure.com/story/12-astrology-houses-meaning Copy Right 2021 by Conde Nast\Allure.

Your natal chart Report. Adapted from, "Just astrology things Free Astrology Birth Chart Report, Free Natal Birth Chart Calcula tor" by Just Astrology Things, 2020, Just astrology things On line. Retrieved August 20, 2021, from https://justastrologyth-ings.com//pages/chart/index.php. Copyrights 2020 by Just Astrology things.

Book

Woodwell, Donna. The Astrology dictionary cosmic knowledge from A-Z, Simon and Schuster, 2019 "Natal chart is an astrology chart that is a stylized map of the sky, predicting by position of the sun, moon, and planets as viewed from a particular time and placements on the earth. Or spiritual intentions of a given moment in time. The cosmic material in which an incarnated soul is clothed (Woodwell 24).

Woodwell, Donna. The Astrology dictionary cosmic knowledge from A-Z, Simon and Schuster, 2019 "Rising sign, noun The Zodiac sign in which the ascendant of a chart is located, the rising sign indicates physical form, personal style and lifestyle (Woodwell 67).

Woodwell, Donna. The Astrology dictionary cosmic knowledge from A-Z, Simon and Schuster, 2019 "Moon sign, noun a Zodiac sign in which the moon is located within, your moon sign indicates how you feel safe and comfortable, what your emotional outlook is, how you form habits and how you're subconscious mind works (Woodwell 53).

Websites

Astrology Answers." Astrology definition", 2021. Accessed September 2021, astrologyanswers.com/ astrology- definitions.

Corinne Lane. "12 Astrological Houses – Astrology Lesson 4" As trology Library. Astrology Library, 19 Aug. 2009. Web. 8 Sep. 2021. <https://astrolibrary.org/houses/>

Patricia Lantz." Natal Chart Symbols and What They Mean" Love ToKnow August 9, 2019. Accessed October 15, 2019. https:// horoscopes.lovetoknow.com|.

David Avocado Wolfe 2016, This is what God said to each of the Zodi ac Signs, accessed September 2021, https:// www.davidwolfe. com/god-said-zodiac-signs/.

Chapter Three: The curse of Inadequacy

David Avocado Wolfe 2016, This is what God said to each of the Zodiac Signs, accessed September 2021, https:// www.davidwolfe.com/god-said-zodiac-signs/.

Chapter Four: Beautiful PERSON-ality

Russ Hudson- co-founder and contributing innovator of The Enneagram

Websites

Clover Leaf 2013, What is an Enneagram? Accessed September 2021, https://cloverleaf.me>enneagram.

Enneagram Institute 2021, The 9 personalities Accessed September 2021, https://www.enneagraminstitute.com/

The Myers-Briggs company 2021, Myers-Briggs Type Indicator® (MBTI®) Official Myers Briggs Personality Test. Accessed October 2021, https://www.themyersbriggs.com

The Myers & Briggs Foundation 2021, More About Personality Type. October 2021, https://www.myersbriggs.org.

Charts

Enneagram 9 personality chart. Adapted from. "The 5 Best Enneagram Resources to Get You Started", by J. P. Heap, March 5 2018, Medium Online. Retrieved September 28, 2021, from https://justinpheap.medium.com. Copy Rights 2018 by J. P. Heap.

Sixteen combinations of the Four preferences of Myers-Briggs results Chart. Adapted from "What Does the Myers-Briggs Personality Test Say About Your Productivity?" by focus Team, 12 April 2018, FocusME online. Retrieved September 30, 2021 from https:// focusme.com/blog/what-does-myers-briggs -personality-test-say-about productivity. Copy Rights 2021 by FocusMe

Chapter Five: Foundated

Nelson Ze Pequeno- a brilliant man, artist, plant dad and creator of Black Menwith Gardens on Instagram platform

Chapter Six: Taken'd Time

Websites

Pinterest 2021, What is Pinterest Help, Accessed September 28, 2021, https://help.pinterest.com>guide

Chapter Seven: Upcycling, Meeting where we are

"Algorithms." Merriam-Webster.com Dictionary, Merriam-Webster, https://www.merriam-webster.com/dictionary/manifest. Ac cessed 29 Sept. 2021

Chapter Eight: Present of Gratitude
Chapter Nine: Manifestation-ing

Memes

"Living with gratitude ..."[Sunset] meme. Meme.com, February 6, 2013. Https//:me.me.com

Websites

"Manifest." Merriam-Webster.com Dictionary, Merriam-Webster, https://www.merriam-webster.com/dictionary/manifest. Accessed 29 Sept. 2021

"The best way to predict the future is to create it" meme. Pin on manifestation machine   memes, Pinterest. August 25,2017, datavatic.com

Chapter Ten: Journeyed & Beyond

"Journey." Merriam-Webster.com Dictionary, Merriam-Webster, https://www.merriam-webster.com/dictionary/journey. Accessed 3 Oct. 2021

"Purpose." Merriam-Webster.com Dictionary, Merriam-Webster, https://www.merriam-webster.com/dictionary/purpose. Accessed 30 Sept. 2021

"Self." Merriam-Webster.com Dictionary, Merriam-Webster, https://www.merriam-webster.com/dictionary/self. Accessed 30 Oct. 2021.

"Soul." Merriam-Webster.com Dictionary, Merriam-Webster, https://www.merriam-webster.com/dictionary/soul. Accessed 30 Sept. 2021.

INDEX

ACKNOWLEDGEMENTS

I want to thank every individual that has been written and beautifully chosen to be in my life. My ENTIRE FAMILY, every teacher I have ever had and every person I have dated, or have talked to throughout my life. My cousins that formed a Family within a family....the instant connection and support we have for one another is remarkable and not one of you made me feel like what I was saying was crazy, if anything Y'all made me feel like I was making the most sense even when I didn't! Thank you to all the young men that came into my life as well. We were not meant to be but I learned so much of myself and of love during our time of coexistence. Literally, I was lucky to find so many men of color that dove deeply, that was vulnerable about their journey to self and through the attempt to love me, showed me I'm worth loving. Finally, thank you to my late Grandfather, Charles Powell...as I write this, I can't help the tears from falling...THANK YOU for letting me just, Be. You shield me from the consequences of being the first "black sheep" of the family. Never did you snuff out my flame, you saw the beauty in my odd thinking even when I said my favorite flower was a Dandelion, a weed. I am so proud of your DNA flowing within me every single moment. You gave me the greatest gift, allowing me to be me...so I can later allow it myself.

"I was pregnant with my second child
and living with my dad for the second time.
One day I was just angry...angry at the lonely
feeling and I remember crying so hard that not a
sound came out. After that, I just stop crying ;
stared at the mirror and began to do my hair,
pulled out some jewelry I never wore and did my
makeup. I had set a "look" that I wanted to replace
everything, both outside and inside. I refused to
feel that pain again. That's when it happened."
-tee

"I was watching a
bunch of Anime
that had
spiritually in it,
that's when it
happened."
-Tygee

TRUST

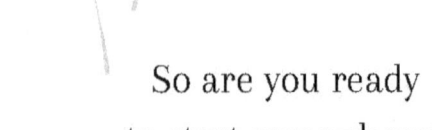

the timing of your life

"It was my 30th birthday and I woke up on
my mom's couch. Me, my mom, TyTy, and Deuce
(our dog). That's when it hit me...like a ton of bricks "
-Damon Wilson

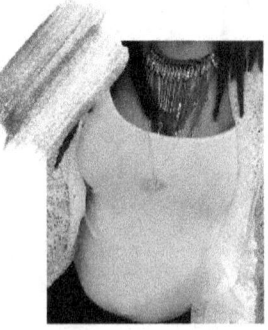

So are you ready
to start somewhere?

Tiffany Kimbrough is "An author, a 'spiritual guru' and photosynthesis manager and a baddie. Black Women can truly do it all". Overall she's a single mother, a humble creative Californian who took the years of studies that filled journals of about 2,000 pages of her own journey to Self and put it into a book.

www.ingramcontent.com/pod-product-compliance
Lightning Source LLC
Chambersburg PA
CBHW060535130626
46553CB00002B/767